Your Space

Workbook 2

Martyn Hobbs and Julia Starr Keddle

CAMBRIDGE
UNIVERSITY PRESS

CAMBRIDGE
UNIVERSITY PRESS

University Printing House, Cambridge CB2 8BS, United Kingdom

One Liberty Plaza, 20th Floor, New York, NY 10006, USA

477 Williamstown Road, Port Melbourne, VIC 3207, Australia

314–321, 3rd Floor, Plot 3, Splendor Forum, Jasola District Centre, New Delhi – 110025, India

79 Anson Road, #06–04/06, Singapore 079906

Cambridge University Press is part of the University of Cambridge.

It furthers the University's mission by disseminating knowledge in the pursuit of education, learning and research at the highest international levels of excellence.

www.cambridge.org
Information on this title: www.cambridge.org/9780521729291

© Cambridge University Press 2012

First published 2012

20 19 18 17

Printed in Malaysia by Vivar Printing

A catalogue record for this publication is available from the British Library

ISBN 978-0-521-72929-1 Workbook with Audio CD, Level 2
ISBN 978-0-521-72928-4 Student's Book, Level 2
ISBN 978-0-521-72930-7 Teacher's Book, Level 2
ISBN 978-0-521-72932-1 Class Audio CDs (3), Level 2

Contents

1 Look at the pictures and write about Owen's daily routine.

Owen's blog space

Hi! I've got a new camera phone. Take a look at my day in pictures.

Owen gets up at quarter to seven in the morning.

2 Write ten sentences about your weekly routine. Use *usually* or *often* if necessary.

play computer games   surf the web   go swimming   play football

collect things   listen to music   play a musical instrument   meet friends

go shopping   read books   play tennis   send text messages   play basketball

Monday   Tuesday   Wednesday   Thursday   Friday   Saturday   Sunday

at the weekend   in the evening   before I go to school

at school   when I get home from school

I often play computer games at the weekend.
I usually go swimming on Sunday.
I play a musical instrument on Thursday evening.

Present simple

1 Complete the sentences with the present simple of the verbs in brackets.

1 I ......*go*...... (go) to my piano lesson on Fridays.

2 He .... (not have) breakfast.

3 We .... (not get) the bus to school.

4 **A** .... you .... (watch) TV in the evening? **B** Yes, I ....

5 My parents .... (get up) late at the weekend.

6 **A** .... Isabelle .... (wear) trainers to school?
B No, she ....

7 **A** How many text messages .... you .... (send)? **B** About ten a day.

8 Carlo .... (not like) classical music.

2 Look at the timetable and write about Henry's week.

1	Monday	orchestra
2	Tuesday	Maths lesson
3	Wednesday	Computer Club
4	Thursday	theatre group
5	Friday	football with Max and Toby
6	Saturday	tidy room
7	Sunday	violin practice

1 On Mondays he plays in the orchestra. (play)

2 .... (have)

3 .... (go)

4 .... (act)

5 .... (play)

6 .... (tidy)

7 .... (do)

3 Complete the questions and answers.

Hi, I'm David

1
.... they know each other?
No, they ....

您好

2
.... Jane speak Chinese?
.... , she does.

ENGLISH

3
Do we .... Maths now?
No, we ....
We have English.

23 × 4 = 92
2a + 2b = c

4
Does he .... English?
No, he .... He teaches Maths.

4 Write the questions. Then write short answers for you.

1 you / send / a lot of text messages

2 your school / have / a computer room

3 you / have / a lot of homework

4 your best friend / play / the guitar

5 Write sentences about you and your life. Use the present simple.

friends · town/city · dad · pet · sister · brother · mum · school

like · play · have · read · listen · do · watch · speak · eat · drink · go · work

My friends and I like computer games. We're very good at them!

Countable / uncountable

6 Write the words in the correct column. Write countable nouns in the plural form.

> water grape chicken bread tomato yoghurt banana orange juice crisp apple biscuit cheese

countable	uncountable
grapes	water

7 Complete the conversation with *some* and *any*.

Sarah Let's make a shopping list. Is there ¹ _any_ fruit?

Alex There are ² _____ bananas and ³ _____ grapes. But there aren't ⁴ _____ apples.

Sarah OK – we must get ⁵ _____ apples. And is there ⁶ _____ water?

Alex Yes, there is. And there's ⁷ _____ orange juice, too.

Sarah OK. Are there ⁸ _____ biscuits?

Alex No, there aren't. But there are ⁹ _____ crisps.

Sarah Good. And is there ¹⁰ _____ chicken?

Alex Yes, there is. There's a lot. And we've got ¹¹ _____ cheese, too.

Sarah Great. Is there ¹² _____ bread?

Alex No, there isn't. But there are ¹³ _____ tomatoes.

Sarah OK. So we must buy some apples, ¹⁴ _____ biscuits and ¹⁵ _____ bread. Let's go to the supermarket!

too much / too many

8 Circle the correct words.
1 There are **too much** / **too many** apples.
2 There's **too much** / **too many** water in the bath.
3 We have **too much** / **too many** vegetables for dinner.
4 There is **too much** / **too many** ice cream.
5 There is **too much** / **too many** pasta.
6 Have you got **too much** / **too many** sausages?

9 Look at the picture of Sandra's room and write sentences with *too much* and *too many*.

bags   perfume   jewellery   pens   T-shirts   paper

1 She's got too many pens.
2 _____
3 _____
4 _____
5 _____
6 _____

1 Complete the names of jobs in the house.

1 m a k e your b e d   **2** m _ _ e _ rea _ a _ t   **3** w _ s _ the _ _ i _ he _   **4** _ ay the _ a _ le

5 pu _ _ ou _ _ the _ _ ub _ i _ h   **6** _ i _ y your _ _ o _ m   **7** c _ ea _ the t _ b _ e

2 🔘 **02** Complete the conversations and match with the pictures. Then listen and check.

| tidying   make   cleaning   doing   calling |
| read   often   ~~watching~~   watch |

A ☐

B ☐

C ☐

1 Ella Are you **1** watching TV?

Mel No, I'm not. I'm listening to music. I don't usually **2** _____ TV in the evening. There are never any good programmes!

Ella I agree! That's why I'm **3** _____ you.

2 Mark Hi David! What are you **4** _____ ?

David I'm reading a book. I **5** _____ read books.

Mark I never **6** _____ books. I usually read blogs!

3 Mum Why are you **7** _____ the kitchen? You never do that!

Ayden I'm not tidying it! I'm **8** _____ my football boots.

Mum You always **9** _____ a mess! Take your boots outside!

Chat zone

🔘 **03** Complete the conversations with the expressions. Then listen and check.

| Are you in trouble?   That's a brilliant idea.   Come on! |

1 Emma I'm bored.

Alyssa Let's go to the park and play football!

Emma _____

2 Liam We're late for school!

Andy OK!

3 Adam It's time to go home! Why are you at your desk?

_____

Lily No, I'm not. I'm doing a project for tomorrow.

Ⓡ **Present continuous**

1 Answer the questions using the information.

1 Is Lee drinking? (✗ – eat)
No, he isn't. He's eating.

2 Are Sandra and Diana playing chess?
(✗ – play computer games)

3 Is Luisa writing? (✗ – read a magazine)

4 Are Joel and Robbie playing computer games? (✗ – play chess)

5 Is Ahmad sending a text message?
(✗ – talk on his mobile phone)

6 Is Lara eating? (✗ – drink)

Present simple / present continuous

2 Circle the correct words.

1 I **'m sending** / **send** my friend an e-card. It's her birthday!

2 The sun **shines** / **'s shining** now. It's a beautiful day for a picnic!

3 Every Saturday I **watch** / **'m watching** a DVD with my best friend.

4 Mum **makes** / **'s making** chocolate cake. Mmm! It smells good!

5 The Geography teacher always **is giving** / **gives** us too much homework.

6 I **'m preparing** / **prepare** the music for my party this evening right now.

7 Every Thursday Anton **plays** / **is playing** the guitar in the school band.

3 Look at the table and write sentences about each person.

Name	Job	Usually	At the moment
1 Alex	teacher	talk to students	listen to music
2 Jacob	bus driver	drive a bus	drive a car
3 Eve	hairdresser	cut hair	paint a picture
4 Sanjay	office worker	send emails	write a letter
5 Joe	farmer	work outside	work in his office
6 Amber	police officer	wear a uniform	wear a party dress

1 Alex is a teacher. He usually talks to students. But at the moment he's listening to music.

2 _____

3 _____

4 _____

5 _____

6 _____

can

4 Look at the things Maria can and can't do. Then write sentences.

can	can't
play football	speak French
play the piano	sing
use a computer	cook
design a web page	draw a picture
do puzzles	make a cake

1 Maria can play football but she can't speak French.

5 **Match the verbs with the pictures. Then write questions and answers.**

speak Chinese ☐1☐   cook ☐

dance a tango ☐   ride a horse ☐

juggle ☐   ski ☐

1

你叫什么名字？

Julie

2

Bill

3

Maria

4

Nick

5

Tommy

6

Pete   Marina

1 Can Julie speak Chinese?
Yes, she can.

2 Can Bill juggle?
No, he can't.

3 ....

4 ....

5 ....

6 ....

very / really / quite

6 **Complete the sentences with *very/ really/quite*. Sometimes there is more than one possible answer.**

1 She's ....*quite*.... good at Maths. She got 60 per cent in the test.

2 She's .... good at English. She got 90 per cent in the final exam.

3 Those trainers are .... expensive. They're 40 euros.

4 Those jeans are .... expensive. They cost 150 euros!

5 Today it's 39°C. That's .... hot!

6 It was .... hot yesterday. It was 22°C.

Communication

🔘 **04** **Complete the conversations. Then listen and check.**

| excuse | say | mean | repeat | spell |

1

Teacher How do you ¹....................... 'boat' in English, Megan?

Megan B-O-A-T.

Teacher Well done!

2

Paola Excuse me. What does 'sailing' ²....................... in English?

Teacher It's when you go on a lake or on the sea in a boat.

Paola And how do you ³....................... 'a very big boat' in English?

Teacher You say 'ship'.

3

Teacher Now open your books and do Exercise 4.

Joe ⁴....................... me, Sir. Can you ⁵.......................that, please?

Teacher Yes, of course. Open your books and do Exercise 4.

Reading

1 **Read the web page and complete the sentences. Circle the correct words.**

1 Sonia lives ...   **a** on a boat.   **b on an island.**   **c** in a school.
2 She is ...   **a** short with dark hair.   **b** short with green eyes.   **c** tall with dark hair.
3 She and her brother go to school ...   **a** by bus.   **b** on foot.   **c** by boat.
4 On the journey to school Sonia's brother usually ...   **a** rows the boat.   **b** does his homework.
   c fishes.
5 The school has got ...   **a** chairs, desks and computers.   **b** chairs and desks.   **c** computers.
6 The students are doing a project about ...   **a** Kashmir.   **b** the lake.   **c** computers.
7 The students sometimes have ...   **a** boat races.   **b** swimming competitions.
   c cricket matches.
8 Sonia likes ...   **a** fishing.   **b** playing cricket.   **c** cleaning.

○○○
◄ ► C + ● http://yourspace.cambridge.org   · Q-

Unusual school routines!

This week we focus on schools in INDIA.

Hi! My name's Sonia and I live on an island on Dal Lake, Kashmir, India. I'm tall and slim with dark hair and green eyes. Every morning I put on my school uniform – a blue dress and a white headscarf. Then I have breakfast and wait for my brother – he can never find his school uniform (black trousers and a blue shirt). He's short with dark hair and brown eyes.

We are lucky because in my village many people don't go to school. We don't go to school by bus, we go by boat! I usually row, while my brother does his homework!

At school, we don't have chairs or desks – we sit on the floor. We study subjects like Maths, Science and Languages. I haven't got a computer at home, but I love playing computer games at school. And we are doing a project on how to keep the lake clean. Sometimes we have school boat races – it's fun!

At the end of the day we row home and play games. My brother often goes fishing, but I like playing cricket. When I grow up I want to be a doctor.

2 **Read the web page again and find ...**

(adjectives to describe people)   _tall_ ....

(clothes)   ....

(transport)   ....

(furniture)   ....

(school subjects)   ....

Listening

3 ○ **05** Listen to Manu. Are the sentences true (*T*) or false (*F*)?

1 Manu lives in a big city called Mumbai. *T*
2 He has got a TV and a computer at home. ....
3 His school is on a train. ....
4 He studies reading, writing and Maths. ....
5 The students don't do Music. ....
6 Manu loves reading books. ....
7 Manu wants to be a doctor. ....

Writing

4 Write about you and your life.

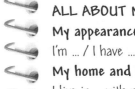

ALL ABOUT ME
My appearance and personality
I'm … / I have …
My home and family
I live in … with my … .
My routine
I get up at … / I go to school … / We study …
My free time
In the afternoon I … / In the evening I … / At the weekend I …
My interests and favourite things
I love … / I can … / My favourite …

Writing focus

Don't forget to check the spelling and punctuation.
Remember:
love/like + *-ing*
I can + infinitive

Your progress

Look at Student's Book Unit 1. Circle: ☹ = not very well ☺ = quite well 😎 = very well

I can talk about my life, my interests and the sports I do.	☹ ☺ 😎	p9
I can talk about the present – where I am and what I am doing.	☹ ☺ 😎	p13
I can describe my friends and family.	☹ ☺ 😎	p16
I can listen to a personal description and understand the main points.	☹ ☺ 😎	p17
I can write a description of my friend.	☹ ☺ 😎	p17
I can ask for the meaning of words, ask about spelling, ask people to speak slowly and repeat things.	☹ ☺ 😎	p108

Your project: personal profile

- Write four short paragraphs about you with these headings:
  1 **facts** name, age, nationality, home town, family
  2 **personal description** appearance and personality
  3 **about me** interests and skills
  4 **about my life** daily routine
- Make a poster. Use photos or drawings to illustrate the paragraphs.

1 Look at the pictures and complete the crossword.

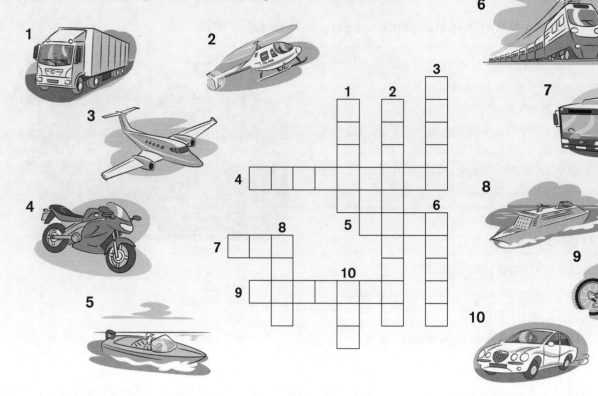

2 🔘 **06** Complete the conversations with these sentences. Then listen and check.

a Were there any good TV programmes on last night?
b Were you at the theatre group last night?
c Where was she?
d Where were you and Danny?

1 Leo ....
Rosie Yes, I was. We're doing a new play. There was a lot to do.

2 Jacob ....
Gregor No, there weren't. It was terrible!

3 Steph ....
Jenna We were in the park with our new dog.

4 Nicole My mum was in the USA last week.
Kyle Really? ....
Nicole She was in Chicago.

Chat zone

🔘 **07** Complete the conversations with the expressions. Then listen and check.

> I've got loads
> This morning was a disaster.
> That's so unlucky!

1 Nicole Hi! How are you?
Danny OK, but .... of homework. Maths, English and Science!

2 Jenna Yesterday was my birthday, but I was ill.
Gregor Oh dear. .... I hope you feel better soon.

3 Rosie Are you OK?
Leo No, I'm not. .... I was late for school. And the teacher was angry.

Past simple – be

1 Put the words in the correct order to make sentences.

1 sunny / was / it / day / a
It was a sunny day.

2 at / bed / 9 am / in / Dan / was

3 was / the / on / 11 am / at / internet / he

4 the / parents / garden / were / his / in

5 there / barbecue / was / a

2 Complete the sentences with *was*, *were*, *wasn't* or *weren't*.

1 I ___was___ on holiday in Mexico last year. (✓)

2 They _____ late for school today. (✓)

3 We _____ interested in the lesson. (✗)

4 The website _____ perfect. (✓)

5 I _____ on the basketball team. (✗)

6 They _____ in bed early last night. (✗)

7 Mum and Dad _____ pleased with me. (✗)

3 Correct the sentences. Then match the pictures with the sentences.

> footballer   scientist   ~~writer~~
> actor   artist   singer

1 Shakespeare was a rock star.
Shakespeare wasn't a rock star. He was a writer. ☐

2 Elvis Presley and Michael Jackson were footballers. ☐

3 Leonardo da Vinci was an actor. ☐

4 Marie Curie was a singer. ☐

5 Charlie Chaplin and Marlon Brando were pilots. ☐

6 Pelé was an inventor. ☐

4 Write questions and short answers.

1 concert / good? (✓)
Was the concert good? Yes, it was.

2 English test / easy? (✗)

3 you / at the disco? (✗)

4 your mum and dad / at the meeting? (✓)

5 lesson / interesting? (✓)

6 they / in the computer room? (✓)

7 Alex / at the match? (✗)

8 Isa and Leo / at the skate park? (✗)

9 you and Adam / in the library? (✓)

10 the train / late yesterday? (✓)

5 Complete the conversation.

Hannah Hi you two! **1** _Were you_ at Jake's party on Saturday, Elisa?

Elisa Yes, **2** _____ . It was fab!

Hannah **3** _____ there, Jade?

Jade No, **4** _____ . I was at the cinema with Sophie. **5** _____ at the party, Hannah?

Hannah No, **6** _____ . It was my brother's birthday so we went to a restaurant for a meal. **7** _____ Daniel and Sam there?

Elisa Yes, **8** _____ . Sam's new trainers were really cool!

6 Answer the questions for you.

1 Were you at school yesterday?

2 Were you late for school yesterday?

3 Were you in the school canteen yesterday?

4 Was your best friend at school yesterday?

5 Were you at home yesterday evening?

6 Was your homework easy yesterday?

a	b	c	d	e	f

there was / there were

7 Complete Lizzie's blog with the correct form of *there was/were*.

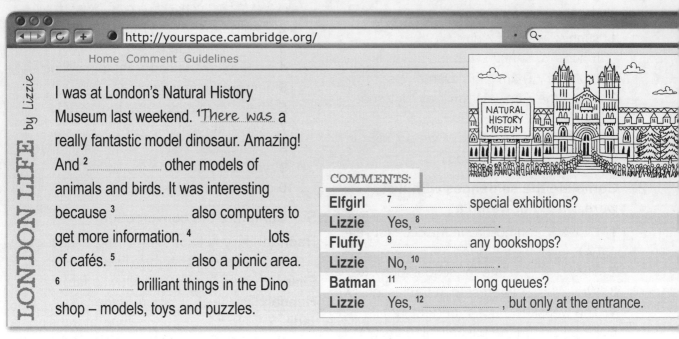

LONDON LIFE by Lizzie

I was at London's Natural History Museum last weekend. [1] There was a really fantastic model dinosaur. Amazing! And [2] .... other models of animals and birds. It was interesting because [3] .... also computers to get more information. [4] .... lots of cafés. [5] .... also a picnic area. [6] .... brilliant things in the Dino shop – models, toys and puzzles.

COMMENTS:

Elfgirl	[7]	special exhibitions?
Lizzie	Yes, [8]	.
Fluffy	[9]	any bookshops?
Lizzie	No, [10]	.
Batman	[11]	long queues?
Lizzie	Yes, [12]	, but only at the entrance.

8 Read the diary and write questions and answers about Lizzie's visit to London.

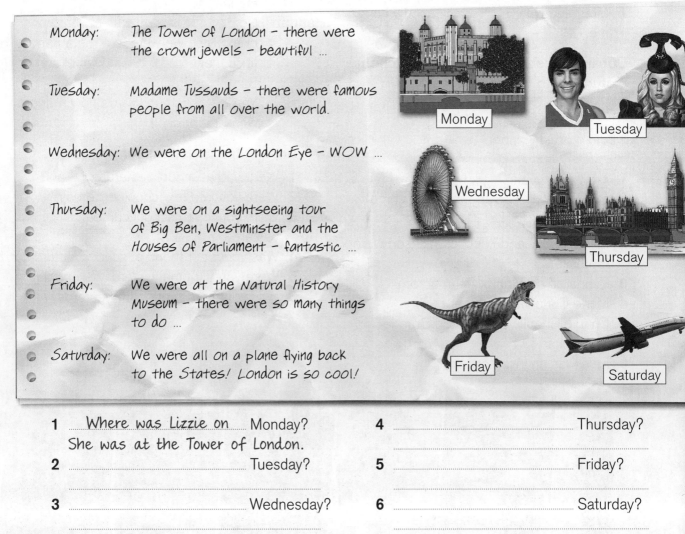

Monday: The Tower of London – there were the crown jewels – beautiful ...

Tuesday: Madame Tussauds – there were famous people from all over the world.

Wednesday: We were on the London Eye – WOW ...

Thursday: We were on a sightseeing tour of Big Ben, Westminster and the Houses of Parliament – fantastic ...

Friday: We were at the Natural History Museum – there were so many things to do ...

Saturday: We were all on a plane flying back to the States! London is so cool!

Monday
Tuesday
Wednesday
Thursday
Friday
Saturday

1 ___Where was Lizzie on___ Monday?
She was at the Tower of London.

2 .... Tuesday?

3 .... Wednesday?

4 .... Thursday?

5 .... Friday?

6 .... Saturday?

1 Where would you hear these announcements and questions? Match them with the places.

a 'Please turn off your mobile phones and put on your seatbelts.'

b 'Flight number 145 from New York. Please collect your bags from belt number 8.'

c 'Flight number 166 for Rio is now boarding. Please have your boarding pass and passport ready.'

d 'Passport, please. Where are you going? How long are you going for?'

e 'Please put your bag here. Give me your ticket and your passport.'

1 at the gate ☐c☐ **2** at passport control ☐
3 at the check-in ☐ **4** at baggage reclaim ☐
5 on the plane ☐

2 There are lots of shops at airports. Match the things with the shops. Then write sentences.

bookshop ☐   sweet shop ☐
music shop ☐   clothes shop ☐
pharmacy ☐   newsagent's ☐   shoe shop ☐1☐

1 We can buy trainers in a shoe shop.

3 ○ 08 Complete the text with the words in the box. Then listen and check.

| burgers   flights   late   gate   player   tired   ~~holiday~~   afternoon   journey   home |

○○○   ✉   ))))

Subject: My holiday in the USA

Hi!
How are you? We are back from our ¹ holiday now. My family and I went to Florida in the USA last month. We had a great time – we visited Disneyland. But we had a terrible ² _____ to Florida! We had an early flight so we left ³ _____ at five o'clock in the morning. We went by taxi to the station. But then we waited for the train to leave because it was very late. Finally it left but it stopped for 15 minutes, and it arrived very ⁴ _____ at the airport! Then we saw lots of queues. There was a problem so all the ⁵ _____ were late. It was crazy! The new departure time for our flight was five o'clock in the ⁶ _____ . We stayed at the airport all day and waited. It was so boring. We ate lots of sandwiches and ⁷ _____ and we looked at the shops. My brother and I played video games and listened to my mp3 ⁸ _____ . Finally we went to our ⁹ _____ and the plane left. We were very ¹⁰ _____ !
Take care,
Lily

Past simple – regular verbs

1 Write the past simple of these verbs. Watch your spelling!

1	study	_studied_	**7**	call
2	decide		**8**	listen
3	plan		**9**	rain
4	wash		**10**	watch
5	travel		**11**	play
6	wait		**12**	arrive

2 Complete the sentences with the past simple of the verbs in Exercise 1.

1 Mum and Dad _decided_ to buy me a new computer.

2 We .... to a song by U2.

3 I .... the party with my best friend.

4 You .... Geography yesterday.

5 Billy .... me on my mobile.

6 She .... for the bus in the rain.

7 They .... volleyball after school.

8 It .... all day yesterday!

9 Sam .... his hair last night.

10 Alex .... home very late.

3 Complete the sentences for you.

Last week ...

1 I called ....

....

2 I walked to ....

....

3 We shopped in ....

....

When I was eight years old ...

4 I liked ....

....

5 I watched ....

....

6 I listened to ....

....

Past simple – irregular verbs

4 Find the past simple forms of these verbs in the word square.

see   swim   give   have   take   come
eat   do   win   go   meet   drive   write
wear   know   lose   ride   find

T	R	A	G	O	Y	L	O	S	T	P	J
W	C	A	M	E	S	T	U	A	R	D	W
W	O	R	I	S	W	A	M	D	E	R	A
E	M	V	E	A	B	E	N	R	T	O	T
K	A	R	T	W	E	N	T	I	O	V	C
N	K	O	F	O	U	N	D	V	O	E	D
E	G	A	V	E	T	N	Q	B	K	S	R
W	R	G	E	T	W	O	R	E	A	R	O
W	A	C	O	R	O	B	U	Y	D	I	D
A	M	E	T	I	N	H	A	D	O	Y	E
T	O	R	O	P	E	N	T	I	E	T	X
C	A	L	W	R	O	T	E	T	A	K	L

5 Match the verbs with their past simple forms.

1 buy	c	**4** wake up	☐	**7** read	☐
2 think	☐	**5** give	☐	**8** put	☐
3 get	☐	**6** drink	☐	**9** forget	☐

a drank	**d** read	**g** gave
b woke up	**e** put	**h** got
c bought	**f** forgot	**i** thought

6 Reorder the letters to complete these sentences.

1 My dad and I **thuhtog** the football match was a disaster. _thought_

2 I **evga** my sister a DVD for her birthday.

....

3 My brother **tuohbg** a new digital camera at the airport. ....

4 I **tgo** top marks in Geography.

....

5 He **koew** up at six o'clock to go jogging.

....

6 I **tofgro** to bring money for the school trip. ....

7 Complete the diary entry with the past simple form of the verbs in brackets.

A disastrous camping holiday

Last summer Rob and Olivia **1** went (go) camping with their parents. They **2** _____ (take) a big tent and lots of food. Mum **3** _____ (drive) and Dad **4** _____ (read) the map. Olivia and Rob **5** _____ (watch) DVDs. But Dad **6** _____ (make) mistakes so the journey took a long time. The weather changed. At the camp site they **7** _____ (put) up their tent in the rain. They **8** _____ (eat) cold food because Dad **9** _____ (forget) the cooker. It was a terrible night. In the morning Olivia **10** _____ (wake up) and **11** _____ (listen) to the rain. She **12** _____ (get washed) but the water was cold! What a holiday! The rain **13** _____ (stop). Rob and his dad **14** _____ (swim) in the sea but the water was cold. Mum **15** _____ (forget) her swimming costume. And Dad **16** _____ (lose) his glasses. Then Mum and Dad **17** _____ (put) the tent in the car and **18** _____ (take) them all to a hotel. They **19** _____ (sleep) in nice beds, they **20** _____ (eat) great food and they **21** _____ (read) books by the pool!

8 Complete the sentences for you.

1 Last year I _____ _____ .

2 Last week my class _____ _____ .

3 Last night my _____ _____ .

4 Yesterday morning _____ _____ .

5 Yesterday afternoon my best friend _____ _____ .

6 Yesterday evening my mum _____ _____ .

7 One month ago _____ _____ .

8 One hour ago _____ _____ .

Communication

⊙ 09 Complete the conversation with the words in the box. Then listen and check.

| have platform single help what please here |

Cashier Good morning. How can I **1** _____ you?
Daniel Can I **2** _____ a ticket to Manchester, **3** _____ ?
Cashier Would you like a **4** _____ or a return?
Daniel A return, please.
Cashier That's £5.50, please.
Daniel **5** _____ you are.
Cashier Thank you.
Daniel **6** _____ time's the next train?
Cashier Let me see. The next train for Manchester leaves at one o'clock.
Daniel What **7** _____ does it leave from?
Cashier It leaves from platform 9.

Reading

1 Read the web page and match the paragraphs with the photos.

http://yourspace.cambridge.org/

Holiday experiences in the USA

Come to the USA and have a great time! We organise adventure and activity holidays for you to enjoy.

A

1 Yellowstone National Park

Trek in the incredible mountains, lakes, rivers and forests of the world's first National Park. Go camping and experience the mountains or try white-water-rafting. See wild animals like bears and wolves.

click here

2 Arizona Desert

Go on a jeep trip and see this amazing desert with its canyons and mountains. Go to the Arizona-Sonora Museum and learn about the incredible desert. Or you can visit Native American sites, or go to Hollywood film sets where they made westerns!

click here

B

C

3 Niagara Falls

See the world-famous 60-metre-high Niagara waterfall on the USA–Canada border. Go down in a lift and see incredible rainbows in the waterfall. You can take a trip in a boat, or go up in a helicopter and see it all from above.

click here

4 Hawaii

You must visit Hawaii. It's got eight wonderful islands, active volcanoes and clear blue seas. There are amazing beaches and you can go swimming, snorkelling or scuba diving on Waikiki Beach. There is amazing sea life so don't forget to go whale watching.

click here

D

2 Read the web page again and answer the questions. Sometimes more than one answer is possible.

Where can you …

1 take a helicopter trip? .... *Niagara Falls* ....

2 see amazing wildlife? ....

3 explore American history? ....

4 do exciting water sports? ....

5 see forests and lakes? ....

Listening

3 🔘 **10** **Listen and match the people with the places in Exercise 1.**

1 Jake		**a** Arizona Desert	
2 Daisy		**b** Niagara Falls	
3 Oliver		**c** Hawaii	
4 Emma		**d** Yellowstone National Park	

4 🔘 **10** **Listen again and correct the sentences.**

1 Jake went on holiday for ~~two weeks~~. *one week*
2 Jake slept in a hotel.
3 Daisy went scuba diving every day.
4 Oliver talked to French people.
5 Emma arrived at eleven o'clock.
6 Emma went in a helicopter.

Writing

5 **Write a postcard about a holiday. Complete the sentences.**

> Hi!
> We went to …
> We stayed in …
> We visited …
> I saw …
> I ate …
> We had a great/terrible time!
> See you soon

Writing focus

Before you begin, take notes. Think of a place and write down all the things you can see and do there.

Your progress

Look at Student's Book Unit 2. Circle: 😟 = **not very well** 🙂 = **quite well** 😄 = **very well**

I can describe past experiences – when I was a child, or last weekend.	😟 🙂 😄	p9 p23
I can talk about travel and transport.	😟 🙂 😄	p22
I can read and understand an account of a holiday.	😟 🙂 😄	p23 p27
I can listen and understand the main points about a holiday.	😟 🙂 😄	p26
I can give a detailed account of my last holiday.	😟 🙂 😄	p27
I can ask for information about places to see and things to do in a town.	😟 🙂 😄	p109

Your project: my holiday

- You went on an exciting three-day holiday. Choose the location and find information and pictures from the internet or magazines.
- Write about the things you did on each day of your holiday.
- Make a poster or a computer presentation.
- Present your holiday to the class.
- Vote on the best holiday.

1 Match the pictures with the animals.

flamingo ☐ hippopotamus ☐ snake ☐1

rhinoceros ☐ giraffe ☐ cheetah ☐

antelope ☐ ostrich ☐

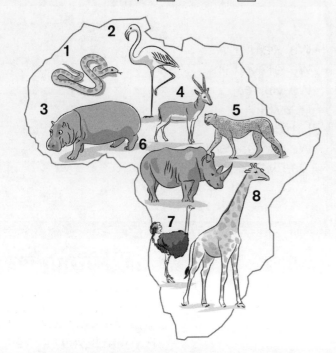

2 What are these animals? The answers are in Exercise 1.

1 It's a large spotty cat with a thin body and long legs. It can run very fast.
.......cheetah.......

2 It likes water. It's a pink bird with long legs. ....

3 It lives in water and eats plants. It's a very large animal. ....

4 It's a large dangerous animal with one horn. It eats plants. It can run fast.
....

5 It's a long thin reptile with no legs. It can be poisonous. ....

6 It's an animal with long legs. It eats grass. It runs very fast and it can jump.
....

7 It's a large bird with a long neck and legs. It can run but it can't fly.
....

8 It's a large animal with a long neck. It eats leaves. ....

3 Match the headlines with the news stories.

1 **Explosion at the factory**

2 **Hurricane hits Florida**

3 **People saved from fire**

4 **Accidents at home!**

5 **Terrible floods in India**

6 **Rock star car crash**

A It started at six o'clock yesterday and destroyed houses and trees.

B After days of rain, thousands of people used boats to escape from their houses.

C **Firefighters rescued five families from their flats yesterday. One person is in hospital but he isn't badly hurt.**

D Lenny Stardust had a lucky escape. His BMW car hit a tree, but he wasn't hurt.

E A new study says our homes are dangerous. Don't stand on chairs. Be careful on the stairs.

F On Sunday night residents of Rochester heard a very loud bang. Luckily there was no one at work.

Past simple – negative

1 **Write negative sentences.**

1 Lizzie visited a museum yesterday.
   Lizzie didn't visit a museum yesterday.
2 We saw my aunt and uncle last week.
3 I listened to Shakira last night.
4 My brother got up early this morning.
5 The students finished the race.
6 Giles sent me a text message.

2 **Look at the table. Write sentences about what the friends did yesterday.**

	Ryan	Isabella	Lucas	Lily
🎧	✓	✓	✗	✗
🎨	✗	✗	✓	✓
📷	✗	✓	✗	✓
👙	✓	✗	✓	✗
🍫	✗	✓	✓	✗
📖	✓	✗	✗	✓

1 Lily and Lucas *didn't listen to* music.
2 Ryan and Isabella .... a picture.
3 Lily and Ryan .... chocolate.
4 Lucas .... a book.
5 Ryan .... photos.
6 Lily and Isabella .... swimming.
7 Isabella .... a book.
8 Lucas .... photos.

3 **Complete the sentences with the past simple form of the verbs in brackets.**

1 Bella *didn't do* (not do) her homework yesterday because she ___went___ (go) shopping.
2 Noah .... (not go) on holiday because he .... (break) his leg.
3 Grace .... (not have) sandwiches today because her dad .... (forget) to buy the bread.
4 Natalie .... (not buy) a new pair of trainers because she .... (not have) enough money.
5 Dylan .... (not take) the dog for a walk because he .... (feel) ill.

4 **Read the diary and complete the article.**

Things to do
- go to bed before 10 pm
- eat lots of fruit and vegetables
- run for two hours each day
- do exercise in the gym
- drink lots of milk
- get up early
- go to school by bike

Things not to do
- stay up till midnight
- eat junk food
- sit in front of the TV
- go to the disco on Saturday
- drink cola or fizzy drinks
- get up after 9 am
- take the bus to school

How to be a winner

What was the secret of my success?

That's easy! I ¹ _went_ to bed before 10 pm and I ² _didn't stay up_ till midnight. I ³ .... lots of fruit and vegetables and I ⁴ .... junk food. I ⁵ .... for two hours each day and I ⁶ .... in front of the TV. I ⁷ .... exercise in the gym and I ⁸ .... to the disco on Saturday. I ⁹ .... lots of milk and I ¹⁰ .... cola or fizzy drinks. I ¹¹ .... early and I ¹² .... after 9 am. I ¹³ .... to school by bike and I ¹⁴ .... the bus to school! That's how I won my gold medal!

5 Look at the pictures. Write sentences about last week for you and your family.

ride a bike

go on a bus

write an email

write a text message

go to the beach

Cinema

go to the cinema

see my grandparents

see friends

put out the rubbish

wash the dishes

do a sport

paint or draw

Museum

visit a museum

go for a walk

I rode a bike but I didn't go on a bus. My mum wrote an email and she wrote a text message.
We didn't go to the beach and we didn't go to the cinema.

could

6 Circle the correct words.

1 I **could to play** / **could play** the piano.

2 She **could drives** / **could drive** a car.

3 We **couldn't speak** / **coulds not speak** French.

4 They **could riding** / **could ride** a bike.

5 You **could play** / **could played** football.

6 He **didn't could** / **couldn't use** a computer.

7 Look at the pictures and write sentences about Teresa's family.

1 When he was young my uncle _could use_ a skateboard.

2 When she was young my aunt .... three balls.

3 When she was young my mum .... very fast.

4 When he was young my grandad ....the guitar very well.

5 When she was young my gran .... very well.

6 When he was young my grandad .... trees.

8 Look at the sentences in Exercise 7 again. Write five similar sentences about your family.

When my dad was young, he couldn't use a skateboard.

1 Find these words to describe feelings in the word square.

> ~~happy~~ sad annoyed bored excited hungry worried thirsty upset embarrassed tired scared

S	A	H	A	P	S	Z	U	T	U	W
C	I	U	P	H	A	P	P	Y	P	O
A	N	N	O	Y	E	D	S	T	S	R
R	E	G	R	W	D	O	I	H	S	R
E	Q	R	E	M	T	B	M	I	B	I
D	O	Y	S	O	I	E	X	R	O	E
E	M	B	A	R	R	A	S	S	E	D
R	W	O	N	E	E	V	M	T	K	L
E	O	R	N	H	D	C	J	Y	F	R
D	R	E	X	C	I	T	E	D	X	E
S	A	D	U	N	U	P	S	E	T	D

2 Write the feelings for these pictures.

> angry ~~excited~~ embarrassed scared worried

1 ......excited......

2 ....

3 ....

4 ....

5 ....

3 🔘 11 Complete the conversation with these words. Then listen and check.

> hang out do taste make ~~play~~

Sandra Hi! Did you ¹ ...play... football yesterday?
David No, I didn't.
Sandra What did you ² ....?
David I read my new book about a teen detective.
Sandra All day? Did you ³ .... with any of your friends?
David Yes, I did. I saw Jamie in the afternoon. What about you?
Sandra I made dinner.
David What did you ⁴ ....?
Sandra Tomato pasta.
David Did it ⁵ .... good?
Sandra Yeah. It was delicious!

Chat zone

🔘 12 Complete the conversation with the expressions. Then listen and check.

> At ... place   Oh dear!   It wasn't my fault!
> a bit fed up   What's up?

Ruby ¹ ....
Megan ² ....
Ruby Look at your tennis racquet!
Megan Oh no! Who broke it?

Ruby ³ .... I found it in the back of the car. Do you want to come and play table tennis instead?
Megan Where?
Ruby ⁴ .... Charlie's ....
Megan I don't know. I'm
⁵ ....

Past simple – questions, short answers and question words

1 Write questions and short answers.

1 They played football.
Did they play football?
Yes, they did.

2 They spoke French.
.... ?
....

3 Sandra walked to school.
.... ?
....

4 He listened to his mp3 player.
.... ?
....

5 We used the computer.
.... ?
....

6 I went to school by bike.
.... ?
....

2 Complete the questions with the words in the box.

| send   get up   have   go   ~~eat~~ |
| watch   meet   speak |

1 Did you ___eat___ any sweets yesterday?
2 Did your mum .... TV last night?
3 Did your best friend .... you any texts last week?
4 Did you .... English last week?
5 Did your class .... Maths yesterday?
6 Did you and your best friend .... yesterday?
7 Did you .... early this morning?
8 Did your parents .... to the cinema last weekend?

3 Complete the conversation.

Lea ¹ _Did you_ do the French homework?

Aydin Yes, ² .... It was easy!
³ .... find any websites for the Geography project on Africa?

Lea Yes, ⁴ .... I found a cool site and downloaded loads of photos. ⁵ .... write an article for our poster?

Aydin No, ⁶ .... I'm sorry.

Lea Never mind! ⁷ .... find some paper and pens for our poster?

Aydin Yes, ⁸ ....

Lea Well done! Let's start!

4 Complete the questions with a question word. Then match them with the answers.

1 _What_ did you buy in town?   c
2 .... did you get to the party?
3 .... did you have lunch with?
4 .... did you leave your lunch?
5 .... lesson did you like best?
6 .... did you go after school?
7 .... did you finish your homework?

a It was disgusting! I hate fish.
b My best friends – Chris and Will.
c A new mobile phone. It's fab!
d We went to Music Club.
e I caught the bus with Jasmine.
f After dinner at 10 pm.
g Maths – it's my favourite subject!

5 Answer the questions for you.

1 What did you do last night?
....

2 Where did you go last week?
....

3 Who did you talk to yesterday?
....

4 What did you eat for dinner last night?
....

5 Where did you go on your last holiday?
....

6 Complete the conversation with the past simple form of the verbs in the box.

> do (x2)   enjoy   play   meet   watch
> take   buy   sleep   ~~be~~

Amy   What ¹ ....was.... the journey like, Natasha?

Natasha   Fantastic! I ² .... two films, ³ .... my computer game and then ⁴ .... for five hours!

Hannah   ⁵ .... you really go without your mum and dad?

Natasha   Yes, I ⁶ .... They ⁷ .... me to Heathrow Airport and my aunt and uncle ⁸ .... me at JFK Airport in New York. What an adventure!

Hollie   What did you ⁹ .... most of all?

Natasha   We ¹⁰ .... tickets for a Broadway musical and that was amazing!

7 Are you good at history? Complete the questions with the past simple form of the verbs. Then circle the correct answers.

1 Which country ....did.... (do) Christopher Columbus discover?
   a Japan   (**b** America)   **c** Mongolia
2 Who .... (be) the winner of Wimbledon 2011?
   a Rafael Nadal   **b** Novak Djokovic
   c Roger Federer
3 Where .... (be) the first Olympic Games?
   a Greece   **b** Italy   **c** Spain
4 Which spacecraft first .... (land) on the Moon?
   a Apollo 9   **b** Apollo 11   **c** Apollo 13
5 Cleopatra .... (be) the queen of which country?
   a Iran   **b** Australia   **c** Egypt
6 Who .... (start) the computer company Microsoft?
   a Sylvester Stallone   **b** Bill Gates
   c Steve Jobs

Communication

◉ 13 Complete the conversation. Then listen and check.

> all   then   was   really   next   you

Harry   Hi Jack! I went to Cairo last week!
Jack   ¹ .... ?
Harry   Yes. It was so cool! First of ² .... I saw the Pyramids.
Jack   Lucky ³ .... !
Harry   ⁴ .... I went on a boat trip along the Nile.
Jack   What did you do ⁵ .... ?
Harry   I drank some tap water and was sick! It ⁶ .... terrible!
Jack   Poor you!

Reading

1 Read the article and put the events in the correct order.

A There was an explosion on Apollo 13. ☐

B The astronauts moved to the Lunar Module. ☐

C The astronauts landed back on Earth. ☐

D Jim Lovell, Fred Haise and Jack Swigert left Florida in Apollo 13. ☐ 1

E The astronauts repaired the oxygen container. ☐

F Mission Control sent Apollo 13 towards the Moon. ☐

2 Read the article again and answer the questions.

1 What date did Apollo 13 leave?
   On April 11, 1970

2 Who was ill and didn't go?
   ....

3 Why did they move to the Lunar Module?
   ....

4 What did they use to repair the oxygen container?
   ....

Apollo 13 – a happy ending!

You probably know about Neil Armstrong and Buzz Aldrin – the first men on the Moon. They landed there in the spacecraft Apollo 11 on July 20, 1969. 600 million people watched them! But did you know that other Apollo missions went to the Moon? In fact, Apollo 13 was nearly a disaster.

Apollo 13 left Florida, USA on April 11, 1970. It had two parts – the Command Module and the Lunar Module. There were three astronauts – Jim Lovell, Fred Haise and Jack Swigert. One man, Ken Mattingly, didn't go because he was ill.

After two days, on April 13, there was an explosion. It damaged the Command Module. The astronauts were in danger. They told Mission Control, 'We have a problem here.' There was only enough air for 15 minutes! So they moved to the Lunar Module.

In the Lunar Module there wasn't much power, food, water or air. They couldn't breathe, because the air was bad. But they repaired the oxygen container with a plastic bag and a sock! They could breathe again.

Now they had one big problem. They were 321,800 kilometres from Earth and they didn't have enough power to get back. Mission Control decided to send the astronauts towards the Moon. Then gravity could pull the spacecraft back to Earth without power.

It was a race against time. Back on Earth Ken Mattingly saved his friends' lives, too. The astronauts couldn't use their computers so Ken guided them to Earth. It was very dangerous. But they landed in the Pacific Ocean on April 17 at 1:07 pm. The men were alive – and heroes!

Listening

3 🔘 **14** **Listen and match the activities with the people.**

John   Sam   Mike

Writing focus

Organise your ideas.
Before you begin,
make a *mind-map*:

read a book
|
Saturday — played computer games
|
went shopping

helped in the kitchen
|
Sunday — visited my gran
|
did my homework

Writing

4 Write an email to a penpal about what you did last weekend.

Your progress

Look at Student's Book Unit 3. Circle: ☹ = not very well   ☺ = quite well   😎 = very well

I can read and understand two short narratives about life-savers.	☹	☺	😎	p29
I can ask and answer questions about the past and understand the answers.	☹	☺	😎	p32
I can read an article about British heroes and understand the main points.	☹	☺	😎	p36
I can listen to information about past heroes and identify specific information.	☹	☺	😎	p37
I can write a paragraph about a hero.	☹	☺	😎	p37
I can tell a simple story in the past, linking ideas, giving opinions and responding.	☹	☺	😎	p110

Your project: a story puzzle

- Write a story about a hero. Include an exciting event and a happy ending.
- Divide your story into five parts.
- Copy the parts onto five cards. Mix them up.
- In class, swap your story puzzle with your partner.
- Read the cards and try to put your partner's story in order.

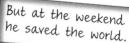

Milo had a secret life –
he was a superhero!

But at the weekend
he saved the world.

1 **Match the pictures with these words. Then write sentences.**

flower bed 7   pond ☐   bird box ☐   gate ☐   fence ☐   path ☐   grass ☐

There is a path. Two girls are walking along the path. They are eating ice cream.

2 **Match the pictures with the sentences.**

Countryside code

Do ...

1 close gates ☐
2 walk on the public paths ☐
3 take your litter home ☐
4 protect animals, birds, flowers and plants ☐

Don't ...

5 climb trees ☐
6 light fires in the forest ☐
7 swim in rivers ☐
8 take stones from the beach [a]

Chat zone

◉ **15** **Complete the conversations with the expressions. Then listen and check.**

| No way!   Anyway   Chill out! |

1 Dylan Oh no! I haven't got the ball so we can't play football! What can we do?

George ....
We can play computer games or watch a DVD!

2 Alfie I've got top marks for my Science test!

Ella .... You're terrible at Science!

3 Isabel Why are you late, Alex?
Alex The bus was late.
.... , the film doesn't start for ten minutes!

Comparative adjectives

1 Write the comparatives of these adjecitives.

1 cold .... colder ....
2 intelligent .... more intelligent ....
3 strong ....
4 expensive ....
5 dirty ....
6 bad ....
7 small ....
8 cheap ....
9 dangerous ....
10 heavy ....
11 big ....
12 noisy ....
13 far ....
14 difficult ....

2 Put the words in the correct order to make sentences. Then match the photos with the sentences.

1 lighter / is / ostrich / an / than / hippopotamus / a
An ostrich is lighter than a hippopotamus. [c]
2 longer / the River Nile / is / than / the River Thames [ ]
3 Tokyo / than / Amsterdam / smaller / is [ ]
4 are / rollerblades / than / a / cheaper / bike [ ]
5 is / than / a / cheetah / tortoise / faster / a [ ]
6 Hawaii / Antarctica / than / hotter / is [ ]

3 Complete the sentences with the comparative form of the adjectives.

light ~~expensive~~ good
dangerous small long

1 A bike's .... more expensive than .... a skateboard.
2 Ricky's .... Mike at French.
3 A giraffe's neck is .... a zebra's neck.
4 An mp3 player is .... a laptop.
5 A pair of trainers is .... a pair of skis.
6 A motorbike is .... a car.

4 Tick (✓) the things you prefer. Then write sentences with comparatives to explain why.

1 (desktop computers)   (laptops) ✓

I like laptops because they are smaller than desktop computers.

2 (cats)   (dogs)

3 (flats)   (houses)

4 (beach holidays)   (adventure holidays)

5 (football)   (tennis)

6 (cycling)   (walking)

7 (horror films)   (romantic comedies)

a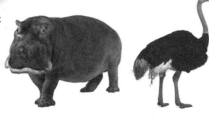

b

c

d

e

f

5 🔘 **16 Complete the sentences in the quiz and decide if they are true (T) or false (F). Then listen and check.**

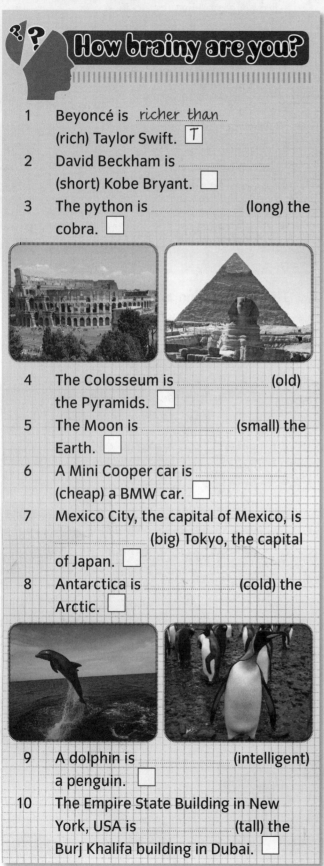

How brainy are you?

1 Beyoncé is *richer than* (rich) Taylor Swift. [T]

2 David Beckham is (short) Kobe Bryant. ☐

3 The python is (long) the cobra. ☐

4 The Colosseum is (old) the Pyramids. ☐

5 The Moon is (small) the Earth. ☐

6 A Mini Cooper car is (cheap) a BMW car. ☐

7 Mexico City, the capital of Mexico, is (big) Tokyo, the capital of Japan. ☐

8 Antarctica is (cold) the Arctic. ☐

9 A dolphin is (intelligent) a penguin. ☐

10 The Empire State Building in New York, USA is (tall) the Burj Khalifa building in Dubai. ☐

as ... as / not as ... as

6 Rewrite the sentences using *as ... as / not as ... as*.

1 Moscow is colder than New York.
New York isn't as cold as Moscow.

2 Vanilla ice cream is nice. Chocolate ice cream is nice, too.
Chocolate ice cream is as nice as vanilla ice cream.

3 An African elephant is smaller than an Indian elephant.

4 A bicycle is more expensive than a skateboard.

5 A cheetah is faster than a lion.

6 Rock music is good. Hip hop music is good, too.

7 Rafael Nadal is younger than Roger Federer.

8 Chess is more difficult than computer games.

7 Write sentences using the comparative and *as ... as*.

1 important / Leonardo da Vinci / Einstein
I think Einstein was more important than Leonardo da Vinci.
I don't think Leonardo da Vinci was as important as Einstein.

2 expensive / computers / mp3 players

3 dirty / cats / dogs

4 fun / skateboarding / swimming

5 beautiful / the London Eye / Big Ben

6 tall / tennis players / basketball players

7 good / Manchester United / Real Madrid

8 interesting / collecting things / reading

1 **Look at the photos and complete the crossword.**

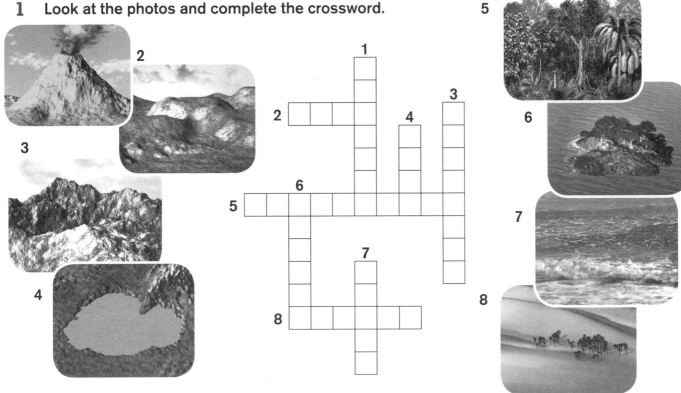

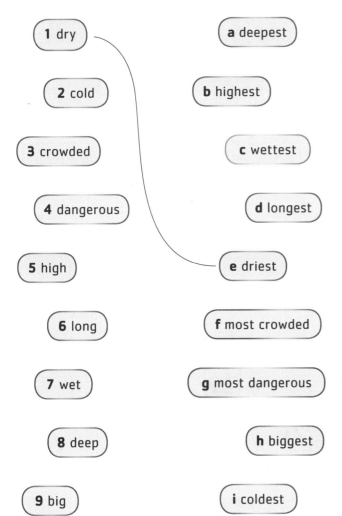

2 🔘17 **Match the adjectives with the superlatives. Then listen and check.**

1 dry	**a** deepest
2 cold	**b** highest
3 crowded	**c** wettest
4 dangerous	**d** longest
5 high	**e** driest
6 long	**f** most crowded
7 wet	**g** most dangerous
8 deep	**h** biggest
9 big	**i** coldest

3 🔘18 **Complete the questions with the correct superlative. Then listen and check.**

1 Who is the .... Olympic runner? (**heaviest / fastest**)
   a Usain Bolt   **b** Asafa Powell
   c Tyson Gay
2 Which is the .... sea animal? (**busiest / most intelligent**)
   a turtle   **b** dolphin   **c** penguin
3 Which is the .... form of transport? (**slowest / deepest**)
   a bus   **b** car   **c** train
4 Which is the .... city? (**most intelligent / busiest**)
   a New York   **b** Washington
   c San Francisco
5 What's the .... sport in the USA? (**most popular / cheapest**)
   a American football   **b** baseball
   c basketball
6 Which film star is the ....? (**shortest / most expensive**)
   a Brad Pitt   **b** Ben Stiller
   c Will Smith

4 🔘19 **Answer the questions in the quiz in Exercise 3. Then listen and check.**

Superlative adjectives

1 Write the superlatives of these adjectives.

1 fast .... the fastest
2 intelligent ... the most intelligent
3 hot ....
4 important ....
5 heavy ....
6 funny ....
7 short ....
8 dangerous ....
9 young ....
10 noisy ....
11 tidy ....
12 expensive ....
13 poisonous ....
14 strange ....

2 Write a table in your exercise book with adjectives you know in the comparative and superlative forms.

Adjective	Comparative	Superlative
long	longer	the longest
difficult	more difficult	the most difficult

3 Complete the sentences with a superlative.

| Maria | Gemma | Camilla |

1 Maria and Gemma have got long hair, but Camilla's hair is ...the longest... .
2 Madison and Olivia have got new mp3 players, but Lily's mp3 player is ....
3 Olivia and Lori's bags are heavy but Gemma's bag is ....
4 Daisy and Niki are good at Maths, but Tania is ....
5 Mr Smith and and Mr Jones are old but Mr Clark is ....
6 Alisha and Tania have got expensive mobile phones, but Chloe's phone is ....
7 Sonia and Lily are intelligent, but Lori is ....
8 Niki and Maria are tall, but Rosie is ....

4 Write superlative sentences about the athletes using the adjectives in brackets.

1 Mirko has the shortest hair. (short hair)
2 .... (tall)
3 .... (heavy)
4 .... (big feet)
5 .... (beautiful)
6 .... (old)
7 .... (small feet)
8 .... (thin)

5 **Answer the questions about your class.**

1 Who is the tallest student?
The tallest student in my class is Tom.

2 Who is the funniest student?

3 Who is the best at Maths?

4 Who's got the longest hair?

5 Who's got the tidiest desk?

6 Who's got the strangest pet?

7 Who is the fastest runner?

8 Who is the noisiest student?

9 Who's got the best handwriting?

6 **Complete the sentences for you.**

MY FAMILY

Who is ...

the oldest?

the youngest?

the most intelligent?

the funniest?

the tallest?

MY POSSESSIONS

What is ...

the smallest?

the oldest?

the most beautiful?

the biggest?

the most expensive?

Communication

🔊 **20** **Complete the conversation with the words in the box. Then listen and check.**

change	please	much	can	excuse	here	have

Simon   ¹............... me.

Shop assistant   How can I help you?

Simon   ²............... I ³............... that red pen, please?

Shop assistant   ⁴............... you are.

Simon   Thank you. How ⁵............... is this computer game?

Shop assistant   That's £30.

Simon   Great. Can I have the pen and the game, ⁶...............?

Shop assistant   That's £33. Here's your ⁷................

Reading

1 Read the article and <u>underline</u>:

1 (the four biggest numbers)   2 (two animals)   3 (three superlative adjectives)

FASCINATING FACTS

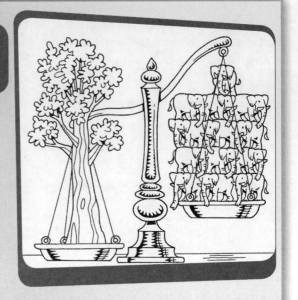

A very old tree!

The biggest tree in the world is in California. It is called General Sherman. It's 83.8 metres tall and it weighs more than 33 African elephants! It is 25 metres around its trunk. Twenty friends could join hands around it! It is between 2,300 and 2,700 years old. It contains enough wood to make 5 billion matchsticks.

Busy bee!

One of the busiest animals in the world is the honey bee! One bee collects 0.8g of honey in its short life of 35 days and flies 20,000 kilometres! Bees in a hive fly 88,000 kilometres and visit two million flowers to make a 500g jar of honey!

The largest passenger ship

The largest passenger ship in the world is *Oasis of the Seas*. The ship is 360 metres long, 65 metres high with 20 floors and 2,706 guest bedrooms. It's longer than four football pitches, and five times larger than the *Titanic*! *Oasis of the Seas* can carry 6,360 passengers and 2,160 crew members – that's over 8,500 people!

2 Read the article again. Are these sentences true (*T*) or false (*F*)?

1 The biggest tree in the world is in Colorado. ___F___
2 The tree weighs more than 33 Indian elephants. _____
3 Twenty people can hold hands around the tree. _____
4 One bee collects 8g of honey in its lifetime. _____
5 A bee lives for 35 days. _____
6 *Oasis of the Seas* is 65 metres long. _____
7 The ship has got four football pitches. _____
8 The ship can carry over 8,500 people. _____

Listening

3 🔘 **21** Listen and ⓒircle the correct answers.

1 The **Kalahari** / **Sahara** is the biggest desert.

2 The Gobi desert is in **North Africa** / **Mongolia and China**.

3 The Kalahari desert is **582,000** / **9,065,000** km².

4 Antarctica is the **highest** / **coldest** desert.

5 Temperatures in hot deserts can be **35** / **45** degrees during the **day** / **night**.

6 Cacti are known as the **flowers** / **trees** of the desert.

7 The kangaroo **cat** / **rat** lives in the desert.

8 People have lived in the deserts for **hundreds** / **thousands** of years.

Writing

4 **Write a description of your class for the school magazine.**

Include information about:
- the number of students in the class.
- your daily routine at school.
- the subjects you study.
- your teachers.
- clubs your class are members of.

> **Writing focus**
>
> Before you write, make notes about all the information. Use these ideas to write your description.

Your progress

Look at Student's Book Unit 4. Circle: ☹ = **not very well** ☺ = **quite well** 😎 = **very well**

I can make comparisons using the comparative and superlative forms.	☹ ☺ 😎	p39 p42
I can give my opinion about things I like.	☹ ☺ 😎	p45
I can understand an article about animals and the environment.	☹ ☺ 😎	p47
I can discuss the issue of litter in a group.	☹ ☺ 😎	p47
I can write a paragraph about the litter problem where I live.	☹ ☺ 😎	p47
I can buy things in a gift shop and ask questions about prices.	☹ ☺ 😎	p111

Your project: an animal Factfile

- Choose an interesting animal and make a factfile poster.
- Look in books or on the internet and find interesting facts about it. Include:
  - where it lives, in which countries and its habitat
  - what it eats and how it finds its food
  - other facts, for example, 'it's got a very long tongue'
  - what we can do to protect it
- Make your poster. Use drawings or photos from the internet.

1 Complete the crossword.

1 There's a lot of water here – you can go swimming.
2 It's got old and interesting things to see.
3 You go and see films here.
4 You do sports and get fit here.
5 You go here to learn. There are lots of teachers and students.
6 You can buy clothes, CDs, books and computer games here!
7 This place is very exciting! There are lots of rides.
8 You can borrow lots of books here and sit and read. But be quiet!
9 It's got trees, grass and paths. You can have a picnic, go skateboarding or play football.
10 Is the fridge empty? Then you can go here and buy food.

2 Choose your three favourite places and write what you enjoy doing there.

I like the library. I choose books and take them home.

3 ⊙ **22 Read the conversation and (circle) the answers. Then listen and check.**

Charlie What are you ¹ **going / doing** this afternoon?
Thomas I'm ² **playing / listening** in a football match.
Charlie Really? What time is the match?
Thomas It's at three o'clock. ³ **Would / Could** you like to come and watch?
Charlie Thanks, Thomas, but I'm ⁴ **going / swimming** to the beach with my mum and my sister.
Thomas Really? Are you going by car?
Charlie Yes, we ⁵ **is / are**. My mum is driving us. We're taking our surfboards. I love surfing!
Thomas Cool!

Chat zone

⊙ **23 Complete the conversations with the expressions. Then listen and check.**

Really?	mad about	Anyway

1 Jim What are you doing tomorrow?
Amber Well ... I'm having a violin lesson, then I'm seeing my friends and then I'm going out for a meal. ...., what about you?
Jim Oh, I'm getting up late and then I'm watching TV!

2 Chloe I'm going to a car show tomorrow.
Archie Do you like cars?
Chloe No, I don't. But my dad is .... them!

3 Jasmine I'm going to a theme park tomorrow night.
Marko ....

Future arrangements

1 Look at the pictures and (circle) the correct answers.

1 Eva (is skateboarding) / isn't skateboarding in the park on Saturday morning.

2 Jodi **is doing** / **isn't doing** her homework after school.

3 We **are going** / **aren't going** to the Sports Club on Friday evening.

4 Yuki and Ben **are playing** / **aren't playing** basketball at ten o'clock on Saturday.

5 Luca **is having** / **isn't having** pizza with friends on Sunday evening.

6 Magda **is making** / **isn't making** a cake for the party on Saturday morning.

7 She **is doing** / **isn't doing** research on the computer in the library tomorrow.

8 Simon **is watching** / **isn't watching** a DVD after school.

2 Answer the questions. Use the prompts.

1 Is Lara going on a safari for her holiday? (go to New York) No, she isn't. She's going to New York.

2 Are Maria and Amanda riding horses on Saturday? (take the dog for a walk)

3 Is Charlie listening to his mp3 after school? (read a book)

4 Is Alberto hanging out with friends in the park on Saturday afternoon? (tidy his bedroom)

5 Are Jack and Mike writing emails to their friends on Sunday afternoon? (watch TV)

3 Look at the poster and complete the conversation.

Have a cool week in the hot summer at our summer camp!

Day	Morning	Afternoon
Monday	Drama Club	play volleyball
Tuesday	Music Club	go swimming
Wednesday	Art Club	play tennis
Thursday	Drama Club	go canoeing
Friday	Music Club	play basketball

Emma Did your mum and dad say you can come to the summer camp next week?

Fran Yes! It's so cool. I **1** 'm doing sports every afternoon.

Emma Me too! I **2** .... on Tuesday, I **3** .... on Thursday and I **4** .... on Friday.

Fran **5** .... you .... to the Drama Club on Thursday morning?

Emma I'm not sure. I'm shy! But I **6** .... certainly .... to the Art Club. Painting's my favourite hobby. **7** .... you .... any musical instruments?

Fran Sure! I **8** .... the guitar in the Music Club on Tuesday morning. I love the theatre too, so I **9** .... to the Drama Club on Monday and Thursday.

Emma Great! The camp's going to be amazing!

4 Put the time expressions in the correct order.

> ~~this morning~~   next month   this afternoon
> tomorrow afternoon   tonight   next year
> tomorrow morning   tomorrow night
> the day after tomorrow   next week

1 _this morning_
2
3
4
5
6
7
8
9
10

5 Write about you and your family's plans.

1 This evening I'm seeing my best friend.
2 Tomorrow afternoon
3 The day after tomorrow
4 Next Saturday
5 The next school holiday
6 Next month

6 Put the words in the correct order to make questions.

1 you / like / orange / juice / an / would / ?
   Would you like an orange juice?
2 cheese sandwich / like / you / a / would / ?
3 you / some / like / would / cereal / ?
4 you / would / come / like / us / to /
   camping / with / ?
5 go / to / like / would / you / swimming / ?
6 some / would / like / strawberries / you / ?
7 on / Helena's party / like / Saturday /
   would / to / you / to / go / ?

7 Look at the pictures and complete the conversations.

1
Jim Would you like some
¹ _crisps_ ?
Tom No, ² .... you.

4
Jim ⁸ .... you
⁹ .... a burger?
Tom No, ¹⁰ .... you.
I'm a vegetarian.

2
Jim Would you
³ .... to go
⁴ .... with
me?
Tom No, I'm sorry. I don't
like sport.

5
Tom ¹¹ .... you
¹² .... some
ice cream?
Jim ¹³ .... , please.
I love ice cream.

3
Jim Would you
⁵ .... to
⁶ .... to the
swimming pool?
Tom No, I'm ⁷ ....
I can't swim!

6
Tom Would ¹⁴ ....
like to ¹⁵ .... a
computer game?
Jim I'd ¹⁶ .... to. It's
my favourite hobby!

1   Write the names of the shops where you can buy:

1 (medicine and make-up)   *pharmacy*

2 (books)

3 (meat)

4 (computer games)

5 (shoes)

6 (fruit and vegetables)

7 (sports clothes)

8 (magazines and newspapers)

2   Match the shopping lists with the shops.

1

2

3

4

a

a TV and film magazine
a newspaper

b
tennis balls
a football shirt
a sports bag

c
a T-shirt
a skirt
a pair of jeans

d
some tomatoes
some apples
a melon

3   🔘 **24**   Listen. Tick (✓) the activities they are sure about and write a question mark (?) for the activities they are not sure about.

1

Alisha
play computer games ☐
hang out in the shopping centre ☐
not buying anything ☐

2

Brandon
meeting friends ☐

3

Caitlin
working ☐
see a film ☐

4   Write sentences about the people in Exercise 3.

1 Alisha *might play computer games* .
2 Alisha
3 Alisha

4 Brandon
5 Caitlin
6 Caitlin

Talking about future plans

1 Circle the correct answers.

1 Jane **is going shopping** / **might go shopping** after school. (✓)

2 We **might see** / **are seeing** a film at the cinema tonight. (**?**)

3 I **may go** / **am going** to the disco on Saturday. (✓)

4 They **are collecting** / **might collect** money for a village in Africa. (**?**)

5 He **is walking** / **might walk** the dog after lunch. (✓)

6 They **aren't going** / **might not go** to the concert. (✗)

2 Write answers to the questions using *may/might* and these expressions.

go this afternoon   have spaghetti bolognese
go early – I'm tired!   do my homework
eat in the canteen
go to a theme park – they're fun!

1 When are you going shopping?
I don't know. I *may go this afternoon.*

2 What are you doing after school?
I don't know. I ....

3 What time are you going to bed?
I don't know. I ....

4 What are you having for dinner?
I don't know. I ....

5 Where are you having lunch?
I don't know. I ....

6 Where are you going on Sunday?
I don't know. I ....

3 Complete the diary for you. Then write sentences with *may/might* or the present continuous.

Monday	go to theatre (?)
Tuesday	visit Grandma and Grandad (✓)
Wednesday	....
Thursday	....
Friday	....
Saturday	....
Sunday	....

1 On Monday I might go to the theatre.
2 On Tuesday I'm visiting Grandma and Grandad.
3 ....
4 ....
5 ....
6 ....
7 ....

Infinitive of purpose

4 Match the sentence halves to make correct sentences.

1 You use an mp3 player
2 I go on the internet
3 She watches DVDs
4 I do my homework
5 We play the guitar
6 They study English

a to speak to people from other countries.
b to listen to music.
c to be in the school band.
d to relax.
e to get good marks at school.
f to find interesting websites.

5 Look at the pictures and write sentences using the prompts.

1 balls / juggle
We use balls to juggle.

4 dictionary / look for new words
....

2 mobile phone / send text messages
....

5 alarm clock / wake us up
....

3 scissors / cut things
....

6 water / cook pasta
....

Communication

○ **25** Complete the conversation with the words in the box. Then listen and check.

| what | can't | like | worry | would | doing | love |

Lauren Hi Mel! What are you ¹ .... on Saturday afternoon?

Mel I'm going to the cinema with my stepmum.

Lauren ² .... are you doing on Saturday morning?

Mel Nothing. I'm free on Saturday morning.

Lauren Would you ³ .... to go shopping with me in the town centre?

Mel Yes, I'd ⁴ .... to. Thanks. I want to buy a new school bag.

Lauren After shopping, ⁵ .... you like to go for a pizza for lunch?

Mel I'm sorry, I ⁶ .... I'm having lunch with my gran.

Lauren Don't ⁷ .... That's OK.

Reading

1 **Read the web page. Where can you do these activities?**

1 see what time it is ☐F☐ **3** buy a second-hand bike ☐ **5** go paddle-boarding ☐
2 watch a sci-fi film ☐ **4** listen to rock music ☐ **6** see *Alice in Wonderland* ☐

What's on in Cambridge this weekend?

Home   Things to do   Where to stay   **What's on?**   Festivals   Shopping   Contact us

A   On the water
It's similar to surfing, canoeing and skateboarding, but it's better! So why not go paddle-boarding? It's new, it's fun, and it's easy! And you can explore beautiful Wicken Fen at the same time.

B   Into the future
Come to the Cambridge Film Festival and see aliens from films like E.T. and Avatar! There are exciting film workshops for 8 to 16 year-olds. You can learn how to do special effects and make-up to create your own film alien. Then you can watch your creation on screen.

C   A very strange world
Alice in Wonderland is one of the strangest and funniest stories ever. There are talking animals, the Mad Hatter (a mad hat-maker) and the horrible Queen of Hearts. The Cambridge Touring Theatre are performing it every evening in the gardens of Wimpole Hall.

D   Let's go shopping
Where can you buy CDs and DVDs, cool clothes, mobile phone accessories, jewellery, books and even second-hand bikes – all in one place? At the Cambridge market on Saturday from 10 am to 4 pm.

E   Come to the fair!
This Saturday is the famous Strawberry Fair, one of the largest free festivals in Europe! At 11 am there is a parade through the city centre. The fair begins at twelve o'clock when the parade arrives at Midsummer Common. There are lots of different types of music and there are also films, a circus, and face-painting! You can buy interesting things at the market stalls, and you can eat food from all around the world.

F   And don't forget the time!
Do you want to know the time? Then you mustn't miss the fabulous 'Grasshopper Clock'. It took seven years and 200 people to make it. Watch the giant insect eat time. It's scary!

2 **Complete the sentences with the words in the box.**

> Midsummer Common   seven years   ~~a new~~   Cambridge market   alien

1 Paddle-boarding is ……*a new*…… sport.
2 At the Cambridge Film Festival you can create your own ……………… .
3 You can buy mobile phone accessories at ……………… .
4 The parade arrives at ……………… and then the fair begins.
5 It took ……………… to make the 'Grasshopper Clock'.

Listening

3 🔘 **26** **Listen and tick (✔) the activities that Joshua, Natalie, Megan and Toby plan to do this week.**

	Joshua	Natalie	Megan	Toby
going shopping	✓			
buying a present				
playing in the school band				
going to the cinema				
going to Steve's party				
playing basketball				
meeting Jamie				

Writing

4 **Think of some interesting things to do and places to visit in your city. Write a short paragraph. Use the example to help you.**

Places to visit and things to do in my city
Places to visit in my city, London, are: Big Ben, The London Eye.
You can take a boat trip on the River Thames.
In the evenings you can go shopping, see a play, go to the cinema or eat in a nice restaurant.

Writing focus

Look closely at the expressions in the example. Use phrases like *You can ...*, *In the evenings ...*

Your progress

Look at Student's Book Unit 5. Circle: ☹ = not very well ☺ = quite well 😎 = very well

I can talk about my plans for next weekend or the evening.	☹ ☺ 😎 p49 p53
I can read and understand teenagers talking about their plans.	☹ ☺ 😎 p53
I can read and understand a brochure about fantastic days out.	☹ ☺ 😎 p56
I can listen to and understand telephone announcements about a museum.	☹ ☺ 😎 p57
I can write an email to a friend about what I did and what I am planning to do.	☹ ☺ 😎 p57
I can make arrangements – invite, accept invitations, apologise and accept apologies.	☹ ☺ 😎 p112

Your project: a tourist brochure

- Choose an interesting museum or place to visit in your town or capital city.
- Look on the internet and find information. Include:
  where it is   what it is   why you should visit   what you can do and see
  ticket prices   opening times   restaurant or café   shop
- Find or draw a map and pictures.
- Make a brochure for tourists.

Museum

1 Match the speech bubbles with the television programmes.

1 comedy [c]   **3** the news ☐   **5** cartoon ☐
2 quiz show ☐   **4** talent show ☐   **6** nature programme ☐

a I want to know what's happening in the world. I watch this programme every day.

d In this programme, teenagers sing, dance or act. It's fun!

b I'm really interested in the environment so I always watch these programmes.

e I always watch this programme with my family. My mum always knows the right answers.

c I watch these programmes to relax. They're really funny.

f I like manga, but my parents like Bugs Bunny and Donald Duck.

2 Write about the three types of programme you like best.

I like comedies because they're very funny. My favourite comedy is Mr Bean.

3 ⊙ **27** Complete the conversations with these words. Then listen and check.

> don't have to eat   ~~have to watch~~
> don't have to do   must come   have to do

Lewis It's time for the football match, Dad.
Dad Sorry, Lewis. I'm watching the news.
Lewis Oh come on, Dad. I **1** _have to watch_ it.
Dad You also **2** _____ your homework.
Lewis I **3** _____ any homework today. Please?
Dad All right then.

Mum Come on, Lewis. Your dinner's ready.
Lewis I'm watching the end of the match, Mum.
Mum You **4** _____ now. Your dinner's on the table.
Lewis I **5** _____ at the table. Can I eat in front of the TV, please?
Mum OK!

Chat zone

⊙ **28** Complete the conversations with the expressions. Then listen and check.

> You can't be serious!   the worst thing
> Cheer up!   That's so unfair!

1 Hugo Can we watch the football?
   Dad Not at the moment. I'm watching the news.
   Hugo _____

2 Daisy What's wrong?
   Kira I've got a History exam tomorrow and _____ is I can't remember any of the dates.
   Daisy _____ Let's go to see that great film about the Ancient Greeks!

3 Millie Listen to this! Tom got 100 per cent in his Maths exam!
   Ethan _____

must / have to

1 (Circle) the correct answer.

1 She **must** / **mustn't** study for the test.

2 They **must** / **mustn't** skateboard in the road.

3 I **must** / **mustn't** leave litter in the park.

4 She **must** / **mustn't** tidy her room.

5 They **must** / **mustn't** eat too much chocolate.

6 We **must** / **mustn't** speak English in class.

2 Read the Youth Club rules and write sentences.

Rules of Farnham Youth Club

You must …

- put away games when you finish.
- pay for drinks at the shop.
- switch off computers after use.
- clean all sports equipment.

You mustn't …

- bring more than two friends to the club.
- leave any rubbish anywhere.
- take animals into the club.
- remove DVDs or CDs from the club.

1 You must put away games when you finish.
2 You mustn't bring more than two friends to the club.
3 ....
4 ....
5 ....
6 ....
7 ....
8 ....

3 Invent five rules for your ideal school.

You must come to school at 10am.

4 Put the words in the correct order to make sentences.

1 has / her / to / room / tidy / Mary
Mary has to tidy her room.

2 early / up / Dad / get / doesn't / to / have

3 clear / have / table / I / the / to

4 school / to / have / go / we / to

5 all / to / speak / have / English / we

6 the / to / doesn't / Jo / rubbish / have / out / put

7 go / have / Saturday / they / on / to / don't / school / to

8 dog / walk / to / the / have / a / for / you / take

5 Look at the table and complete the sentences.

Our camping holiday	Mum and Dad	George	Olivia
tidy the tents			✓
get the water		✓	
go shopping			✓
cook dinner	✓		
wash the dishes		✓	

1 Olivia ____has to____ tidy the tents.
2 George .... go shopping.
3 Mum and Dad .... cook dinner.
4 George .... get the water.
5 Mum and Dad .... wash the dishes.
6 Olivia .... cook dinner.

6 Complete the email with *have to / has to / don't have to / doesn't have to.*

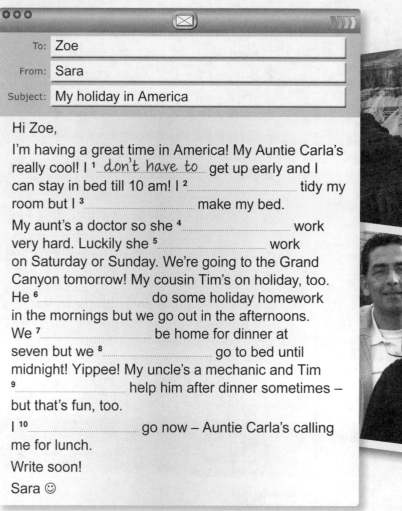

To: Zoe
From: Sara
Subject: My holiday in America

Hi Zoe,

I'm having a great time in America! My Auntie Carla's really cool! I ¹ <u>don't have to</u> get up early and I can stay in bed till 10 am! I ² .... tidy my room but I ³ .... make my bed.

My aunt's a doctor so she ⁴ .... work very hard. Luckily she ⁵ .... work on Saturday or Sunday. We're going to the Grand Canyon tomorrow! My cousin Tim's on holiday, too. He ⁶ .... do some holiday homework in the mornings but we go out in the afternoons. We ⁷ .... be home for dinner at seven but we ⁸ .... go to bed until midnight! Yippee! My uncle's a mechanic and Tim ⁹ .... help him after dinner sometimes – but that's fun, too.

I ¹⁰ .... go now – Auntie Carla's calling me for lunch.

Write soon!

Sara ☺

7 Write questions and short answers.

1 I / make my bed (✓)
Do I have to make my bed?
Yes, you do.
2 Lara and Molly / take the exam (✗)
3 Nick / go to school by bus (✗)
4 Alberto and Sam / meet outside the cinema (✓)
5 you / study this weekend (✓)
6 Grace / have music lessons after school (✓)
7 you / take the dog for a walk every day (✓)
8 Ana / help her brother with his Maths homework (✗)

8 Complete the sentences for you. Use *have to / don't have to.*

1 I .... do my English homework after school.
2 I .... cook dinner tonight.
3 I .... play a musical instrument this year.
4 I .... go to bed before 10 pm tomorrow.
5 I .... do a project at school this week.
6 I .... go to school by bus the day after tomorrow.
7 I .... do a sport next Monday.
8 I .... get up before 6.45 am tomorrow.

1 Find these things in the word square.

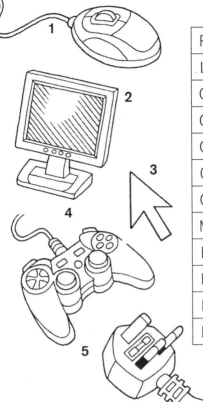

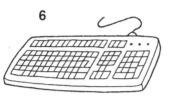

P	R	T	N	J	O	S	T	I	C	C	K
L	K	I	M	O	U	S	E	I	N	T	E
O	E	J	U	Y	M	A	I	C	O	N	E
G	Y	M	O	S	E	I	V	E	R	M	B
G	B	P	R	T	B	O	A	G	H	O	O
C	O	P	R	I	N	T	E	R	I	N	A
O	A	B	E	C	R	U	S	O	R	S	H
M	R	S	S	K	B	S	C	R	E	E	N
P	D	O	Y	J	O	S	T	A	C	M	L
P	L	U	G	E	P	R	M	O	N	A	E
E	I	M	O	N	I	T	O	R	S	T	E
R	S	C	R	C	U	R	S	O	R	R

2 Complete the sentences with words from the word square.

1 Do you like my new _____monitor_____? My old one was big and black. But this one is silver!

2 You need a _____ to play a lot of video games.

3 I like using this _____. It feels really comfortable in my hand.

4 My little brother broke my _____. Now I can't type the letter 'e'.

5 A European or a UK _____ doesn't work in America. They are the wrong shape.

6 I've got a new _____. It's got really good colours so I can print my photos.

7 I can't read the text. Your _____ is really dirty! You have to clean it.

3 ◯ **29 Match the problems with the advice. Then listen and check.**

1 I always feel tired in the morning.
2 I want to play the electric guitar.
3 Mark found £500 in the street.
4 I can't use the internet on my computer today.
5 My brother is really bored.
6 My printer doesn't work. I can't read the text.
7 I feel terrible today.

a You should have music lessons.
b You shouldn't go to school.
c You should change the ink.
d You shouldn't stay up so late.
e He shouldn't watch TV all day.
f He shouldn't keep it.
g You should turn it off and turn it on again.

should

1 **Put the words in the correct order to make sentences.**

1 should / study / I / more
I should study more.

2 shouldn't / watch / he / TV / too / much

3 should / speak / we / English / ?

4 should / yes / we

5 go / bed / late / shouldn't / I / to

6 room / should / they / tidy / the

7 homework / do / he / his / should

8 shouldn't / out / she / late / stay

9 I / now / should / home / go / ?

10 arrive / you / early / should

2 **Complete the sentences with *should* or *shouldn't*.**

1 My penpal ....should.... write me an email. (✓)

2 My sister .... go into my bedroom. (✗)

3 You .... go to the cinema tonight. (✓)

4 The teacher .... give us so much homework. (✗)

5 The dog .... sit on the sofa. (✗)

6 My parents .... buy me a new mobile phone. (✓)

7 An athlete .... eat junk food. (✗)

8 We .... send text messages in class. (✗)

3 **Complete the sentences with *should* or *shouldn't* and these phrases.**

buy this computer	go on the internet	watch this DVD	go to bed late
practise every day	clean your teeth	walk the dog	~~take this medicine~~

1 You should take this medicine and go to bed.

2 You .... every day.

3 You .... for information.

4 You .... in the morning and before you go to bed.

5 You .... when you have school the next day.

6 You .... It's great!

7 You .... Then you can play in the school band.

8 You .... It's too expensive!

Imperative

4 Circle the correct answers.

1 **Don't cross** / Cross the road. It's too busy!

2 Take / **Don't take** food into the library.

3 Close / **Don't close** the door behind you, David!

4 Eat / **Don't eat** ice cream in your favourite T-shirt.

5 **Do** / Don't do your homework! There's a test tomorrow!

6 Tidy / **Don't tidy** that room, Molly. It's a jungle!

7 **Don't speak** / Speak after the test starts.

8 Please **sit down** / don't sit down. Now, how can I help you?

Communication

◉ **30** **Complete the conversation. Then listen and check.**

too   prefer   what   agree   like

Amanda ¹............................. films do you like, Jessica?
Jessica I really like fantasy films. They're great!
Amanda Me ²............................. .
Jessica Do you ³............................. adventure films?
Amanda I love them. They're so cool!
Jessica I ⁴............................. fantasy films. They're more interesting.
Amanda I don't ⁵............................. . Adventure films are the best!

Reading

1 **Read the web page. Are the sentences below true (*T*) or false (*F*)?**

1 Paul isn't any good at sport. ⎯T⎯
2 Izzie loves reality shows. ⎯⎯⎯⎯
3 Amelia's best friend is shy. ⎯⎯⎯⎯
4 Alfie's parents didn't give him an mp3 player. ⎯⎯⎯⎯
5 Daniel likes playing with his little brother. ⎯⎯⎯⎯

○○○ 〈◀▶〉 C + ● http://yourspace.cambridge.org ・ Q-

Dear  Marion

Have you got a problem? Then write to me. I can give you advice.

 **1** My classmates laugh at me because I'm really bad at sport. I can't play football or tennis and I can't catch a ball. Can you help? *Paul*

 **2** I love reality TV shows and I watch them every day. But my best friend wants me to play computer games with her. What should I do? *Izzie*

 **3** My best friend hangs out with lots of people during school breaks. I'm jealous because she's so popular. What should I do? *Amelia*

 **4** I found an mp3 player at school but I didn't give it to the teacher. I took it. Now I say it's a present from my parents. I know I was wrong. Help! *Alfie*

 **5** My little brother's a monster! He comes into my room and plays with my things and breaks them. He also hangs out with me and my friends. It's so unfair. *Daniel*

2 **Read the web page again and match the people with what they might say.**

1 'I'm so unhappy. My friend prefers other people.' ⎯Amelia⎯
2 'I'm sorry, I can't meet you – my favourite programme is on TV.' ⎯⎯⎯⎯
3 'No, thanks. I can't play it.' ⎯⎯⎯⎯
4 'Ben! What are you doing in my room?' ⎯⎯⎯⎯
5 'Do you like it? It was a birthday present.' ⎯⎯⎯⎯

Listening

3 ⏺ **31** Listen and complete the advice with the words in the box. Then match the advice with the problems from the web page on page 50.

| should   brother   play   see   sports   friends   give   ~~honest~~   exercise   shouldn't |

A Yes, you made a mistake. But it isn't too late. You should be ¹ _honest_ . Tell your parents or your teacher and ² .... them the mp3 player. ☐4

B Don't worry! You've got time to watch TV and ³ .... your friends! You should find a day when you can ⁴ .... computer games with her. ☐

C Poor you. You ⁵ .... talk to your parents. But remember your little ⁶ .... isn't a monster – he admires you! Why don't you find time to play with him too? ☐

D I was bad at sport at school, too. But you should do ⁷ .... – it's good for you! Talk to your PE teacher. There are lots of ⁸ .... you can try – running, karate, cycling, skateboarding! ☐

E Cheer up! Your best friend likes you, so you ⁹ .... worry. Why don't you hang out with her during the breaks? You may make some new ¹⁰ .... ! ☐

Writing

4 Write four pieces of advice for each situation.

1 I want to learn English.   *Why don't you ...   You should ...*
2 I want to get fit.
3 I want to make new friends.

Writing focus

Before you begin, note down as many ideas as you can for each situation. Then choose the best ones.

Your progress

Look at Student's Book Unit 6. Circle: ☺ = not very well ☺ = quite well 😎 = very well

I can read a TV guide and understand the main points.	☺ ☺ 😎	p58
I can talk about things I have to do.	☺ ☺ 😎	p59 p61
I can give and understand advice.	☺ ☺ 😎	p64
I can listen to phone messages and make notes.	☺ ☺ 😎	p67
I can write and understand text messages.	☺ ☺ 😎	p67
I can ask for and give opinions about films.	☺ ☺ 😎	p113

Your project: ideal TV evening

- Make an imaginary TV guide for today's TV from 6 pm to 12 pm.
- Choose the types of TV programmes you want to watch and invent names for them.
- Write the times they start and finish and short descriptions for each one.
- Include drawings or photos to illustrate the programmes.
- Put all the TV guides on the classroom wall. Choose the best one.

1 Read the texts and match them with these words.

1 letter [f] **2** instruction manual [ ] **3** note [ ] **4** magazine [ ]
5 website [ ] **6** advert [ ] **7** poster [ ] **8** newspaper [ ]

a Can you call me on my mobile? Thanks! Sacha

b
Your top 10!
☐ music videos
☐ funny films
☐ books and magazines
☐ animals

c
Schoolgirl finds £10,000
Nicole Clarke had a big surprise yesterday. She saw a plastic bag in the road ...

d **Insert a SIM card and battery**
Keep all SIM cards away from small children.
For more information on SIM cards, contact your SIM card vendor.

e
GossipMag
My celebrity week
Mel goes to New York and visits the hottest clubs and meets the coolest people ...

f
Rosy Days Holidays
Greentown
GR3 TWN
14/03
Dear Ms Anderson,
Thank you for your recent phone call. I'm writing today to ask ...

g
FOR SALE
BMX racing bike.
Two years old.
Good condition.
Call Harry on
0223 615496

h
Larry Goldsmith presents
Diamond Life
with support band
live at the Culture Club
Tonight at 8 pm

2 ◉ 32 Complete the diary with the words in the box. Then listen and check.

| was sitting | was wearing | were talking | was feeling | wasn't wearing | was raining |

Monday

What horrible weather! It ¹_____ this morning. I walked to school with Harry. He ²_____ a new blue jacket. Very cool! The first lesson was History. Two of my friends got in trouble with the teacher. They ³_____ all the time! I saw Jack at lunchtime in the canteen. He ⁴_____ his sunglasses today! He ⁵_____ next to Harry. We had Drama in the afternoon. I usually enjoy that but today I ⁶_____ a bit tired. I went to bed very early!

Chat zone

◉ 33 Complete the conversations with the expressions. Then listen and check.

| I can't believe it! Of course! |

1 Nick I've got two tickets for the concert tonight. Do you want one?
Alfie _____ What time does it start?

2 Erin I saw Luke in the town centre today.
Sarah That's great! Did you talk to him?
Erin Well, I said hello, but he walked right past me! _____
Sarah Oh!

Past continuous

1 Complete the sentences with the correct form of the verbs in brackets.

Joe's Blog

Yesterday at 6 pm I was watching a movie at the cinema. What about you and your family? *Joe*

Comments

1 I ...was doing... (do) my homework. Boring! *Alex*

2 My sister and I .... (eat) ice cream in the garden. *Callum*

3 My dad .... (walk) the dog. *Holly*

4 My parents .... (make) dinner and I .... (help) them. *Adam*

5 My little brothers .... (play) basketball. *Leah*

6 I .... (swim) in the outdoor pool near my house. *Ella*

7 My sister Amy .... (send) text messages. *Liam*

8 My mate Tom .... (hang out) at my house. *Julio*

2 Look at the picture and complete the sentences using the past continuous and the phrases in the box.

read a newspaper   write an email
ride a bike   rollerblade
feed the ducks   sail on the lake
play computer games   sit under a tree

1 George was riding a bike.
2 Alice and Lucy ....
3 ....
4 ....
5 ....
6 ....
7 ....
8 ....

3 Look at the picture again and write what the people were *not* doing.

1 George wasn't feeding the ducks.
2 Alice and Lucy ....
3 ....
4 ....
5 ....
6 ....
7 ....
8 ....

4 Reorder the words to make questions. Then answer the questions for you.

1 doing / yesterday afternoon / were / at 2.30 / you / what / ?
What were you doing at 2.30 yesterday afternoon?
I was reading a magazine.

2 on Saturday / were / what / at 8 pm / doing / you / ?

3 your best friend / what / doing / yesterday morning / was / ?

4 at 3 pm / doing / what / were / on Sunday / your parents / ?

5 doing / your teacher / at ten o'clock / was / what / this morning / ?

6 were / at midnight / last night / doing / what / you / ?

Adverbs of manner

5 Write the adverbs of manner.

1 happy
  happily

2 good

3 busy

4 sad

5 noisy

6 fast

7 angry

8 hard

9 careful

10 slow

6 Complete the sentences. Use adverbs from Exercise 5.

1 Ruby danced ___well___ and won first prize in the contest.

2 The girls shouted _____ at each other.

3 The snail moved _____ across the ground.

4 The birds sang _____ outside my window and woke me up!

5 After the holiday, Amy and Grace _____ waved goodbye.

6 Blondel walked _____ along the high wire.

7 I studied _____ for the test.

8 Jake smiled _____ when he got his new mobile phone.

1 Look at the pictures and complete the sentences with the past simple of the verbs in brackets. Then put them in the correct order.

Toby's terrible day!

He didn't .... (catch) it.

Toby _hit_ (hit) his head on the door. ☐1

Then Toby .... (crash) his car into a tree.

And it .... (destroy) a house!

He .... (drop) his favourite coffee cup.

And he .... (break) his favourite cup!

The tree .... (fall) down.

Toby didn't .... (lift) the tree. It was too heavy!

Poor Toby!

2 ◯ **34** Complete the story with the words in the box. Then listen and check.

| was calling | were chatting | ~~was walking~~ | was looking for | was sitting | was lying |

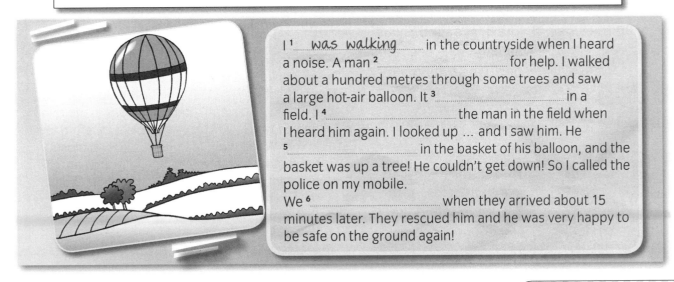

I ¹ _was walking_ in the countryside when I heard a noise. A man ² .... for help. I walked about a hundred metres through some trees and saw a large hot-air balloon. It ³ .... in a field. I ⁴ .... the man in the field when I heard him again. I looked up ... and I saw him. He ⁵ .... in the basket of his balloon, and the basket was up a tree! He couldn't get down! So I called the police on my mobile.
We ⁶ .... when they arrived about 15 minutes later. They rescued him and he was very happy to be safe on the ground again!

Past simple v. past continuous

1 Complete the sentences with the past continuous form of the verbs in brackets.

1 We _were watching_ (watch) TV when Grandma and Grandad arrived.

2 Pete _____ (wash) the dishes when he broke the glass.

3 I _____ (send) a message when the phone rang.

4 _____ you _____ (fly) to Madrid when you lost your passport?

5 Megan _____ (listen) to her mp3 player when the bus arrived.

6 I _____ (hang out) with Laura when I got your text message.

7 _____ you _____ (study) in the library when I called you?

8 Ajay _____ (walk) to the park when he found ten dollars!

2 Look at the pictures and (circle) the correct answers.

1 Jake **ate** / (**was eating**) his breakfast when a bird (**flew**) / **was flying** into the kitchen.

2 Sophie **walked** / **was walking** when she **saw** / **was seeing** a strange light in the sky.

3 The boat **sailed** / **was sailing** in the sea when it **hit** / **was hitting** a rock.

4 They **wore** / **were wearing** T-shirts and jeans when they **met** / **were meeting** the Queen.

3 Complete the conversations with the past continuous or past simple form of the verbs in brackets.

1 A Hi Jane! What _were you doing_ (do) when I _____ (see) you in town yesterday?

 B I _____ (look) for some new jeans.

2 A Why _____ Lea _____ (stand) outside the hospital when I _____ (see) her yesterday afternoon?

 B She _____ (wait) to see a doctor.

3 A Who _____ you _____ (talk) to when I _____ (try) to call you last night?

 B My cousin Jamie in Colorado!

4 A Where _____ they _____ (go) when we _____ (drive) past them in the car yesterday afternoon?

 B They _____ (walk) to the football match.

4 Complete the email with the past continuous or past simple form of the verbs in brackets.

Subject: School trip disaster

Hi Luke!

Guess what? Yesterday we ¹ _went_ (go) on our school trip to the coast – what a disaster!

It ² _____ (rain) so much that it was impossible to see the sea! First we ³ _____ (visit) an old castle near a pretty little town and then we ⁴ _____ (buy) souvenirs in the shops in the town centre. But our teacher ⁵ _____ (fall) over when we ⁶ _____ (run) back to the bus in the rain and so we ⁷ _____ (decide) to return home. When we ⁸ _____ (drive) along the motorway there ⁹ _____ (be) an accident so we ¹⁰ _____ (not get) home until midnight!

See you soon!

Rick

Articles

5 Circle the correct answers.

1 In my dream I had lunch with
the / **an** alien!

2 Every night you can see **the** / **a** Moon
and stars.

3 Agyness Deyn is **the** / **a** famous model.

4 Yesterday I met **the** / **a** friend in the
town centre.

5 How many people are there in **a** / **the**
world?

6 I would love to win **the** / **a** school dance
competition this year.

7 Would you like **a** / **an** apple?

8 I bought **a** / **an** new computer game
yesterday.

6 Complete the sentences with *a/an*, *the*
or no article (–).

1 My mum's ....*a*.... ballerina! I think that's
.... coolest job in the world!

2 My best friend bought .... dog and
.... cat. .... dog's called Woof and
.... cat's called Miaow!

3 In .... Geography we're studying ....
Indians who live in .... Amazonian
rainforest.

4 We did .... Maths test yesterday. It
was .... most difficult test the teacher
could give us!

5 We went to .... new shopping centre
in town and I bought .... new DVD.

6 I bought two .... ice creams yesterday.
.... lemon one was for me and ....
chocolate one was for my friend Liz.

Communication

🔘 **35** Complete the conversations. Then listen and check.

ahead	no	shall	borrow	sorry	can	kind	idea

1
Max   Can I ¹............... your blue pen, please, Teresa?
Teresa   Sure. Go ²............... .
Max   Thanks. That's very ³............... of you.

2
Patty   It's really cold in here!
Lara   ⁴............... I close the window?
Patty   That's a good ⁵............... .

3
Tina   Shall I carry that bag for you?
Nathan   ⁶..............., that's OK. It isn't very heavy.

4
Ayla   ⁷............... I use your mobile phone?
Fay   No, I'm ⁸............... . It's at home.

Reading

1 Read the article and match the paragraphs with the headings.

    a (Successful films) ☐   **b** (A dangerous journey) ☐   **c** (A popular book) ☐

The book of the millennium!

1 Hobbits are short people with hairy feet – they live in comfortable homes underground and love good food. But they don't like danger. The hobbit Frodo has got a problem. Many years ago his uncle, Bilbo Baggins, found a special gold ring. When he got old he gave the ring to Frodo. But now the dark powers of Middle Earth want the ring again. So Frodo, his friends and the wizard Gandalf must leave home and go on a dangerous journey.

2 You may recognise this story. It's the beginning of *The Lord of the Rings* – a fantasy novel. It's a very long novel in three volumes and 1,000 pages. It took 11 years to write! The author, J.R.R. Tolkien, was a professor at Oxford University.

Tolkien wrote the novel over 50 years ago. Now *The Lord of the Rings* is one of the most popular books in the world. Hundreds of millions of people love it – in the UK and Australia they voted it their favourite book.

3 But of course you might know *The Lord of the Rings* films better. These three successful films have incredible special effects, computer-generated battles and amazing music. They won 17 Oscars! The director was Peter Jackson and they were filmed in New Zealand. Many tourists now visit the beautiful film locations. Over 2,000 people worked on the films, including the actors Orlando Bloom, Liv Tyler and Cate Blanchett. The project took eight years to make, 18 months to film and cost $640 million. So what are you waiting for? Watch the DVDs or read the books!

2 Read the article again. Are the sentences below true (*T*) or false (*F*)?

1 Frodo's uncle, Bilbo Baggins, gave him a ring. ....
2 Bilbo, Frodo and his friends go on a journey. ....
3 The author of the novel *The Lord of the Rings* is Peter Jackson. ....
4 There are four films of *The Lord of the Rings*. ....
5 They made the films in New Zealand. ....

3 Match these numbers from the article with the correct information.

1 1,000   **a** years to make the films
2 11   **b** months to film
3 17   **c** people worked on the films
4 2,000   **d** cost of making the films
5 8   **e** pages in the book
6 18   **f** Oscars for the films
7 $640,000,000   **g** years to write the novel

Listening

4 ⊙ **36** **Listen and complete the summary of *The Lord of the Rings* with the words in the box.**

> home   ~~go~~   steals   fire   think   ring   journey   fight

The evil Sauron lives in Mordor and wants to become the Lord of Middle Earth. To do this he must have 'the Ring'.

To destroy the Ring Frodo must ¹........go........ to Mordor and throw the ²................... into the fire at Mount Doom. On the journey to Mordor, Frodo and his friends lose Gandalf and ³................... he is dead. But Gandalf comes back and the friends ⁴................... a terrible battle and win.

Frodo and his friend Sam start their final ⁵................... to Mount Doom in Mordor. After some horrible adventures, a creature called Gollum ⁶................... the Ring. But Gollum falls into the ⁷................... at Mount Doom with the Ring. Middle Earth is safe again. The friends go back ⁸................... and live in peace.

Writing

5 **Write a story using the words below. Decide how the story ends.**

to skateboard   to have a good time   to go too fast   to fall into the lake
to look in the water   to find a diamond bracelet   to decide
to be honest   to take   police station   to receive 50 euros reward

Last Sunday Jo and Tom were skateboarding in the park.
They were having a good time. ...

Writing focus

Check your writing carefully. Pay attention to spelling and punctuation.

Your progress

Look at Student's Book Unit 7. Circle: ☹ = not very well ☺ = quite well 😁 = very well

I can talk about what I was doing in the past.	☹ ☺ 😁	p68 p73
I can read a blog and understand the main events.	☹ ☺ 😁	p69
I can listen to and understand a story and its main events.	☹ ☺ 😁	p76
I can prepare and do an interview.	☹ ☺ 😁	p77
I can write a simple story set in the past.	☹ ☺ 😁	p77
I can ask for permission and offer to do things.	☹ ☺ 😁	p114

Your project: my reading diary

- Make a note of all the different things you read this weekend, for example:
  notice   text message   novel   comic   email   instructions for something   advert
- Write a weekend reading diary. Give lots of information.

> On Saturday I read the sports pages in my dad's newspaper. Then I read three text messages. Two messages were from my friends. The other text message was from my sister. I also read the instructions for my new camera.

- Put all the reading diaries on the classroom wall. Are they very different?
  How many different things did the class read? Who read the most?

1 **Complete the words for jobs. Then match them with the pictures.**

1 s c i e n t i s t   **2** v___t   **3** ___il___t   **4** m___s___c___n   **5** ch_____   **6** ____thl___t____

7 r____c____g dr___v___r   **8** d___t___ct___v____   **9** n___r___e   **10** f____r___fi___h___er

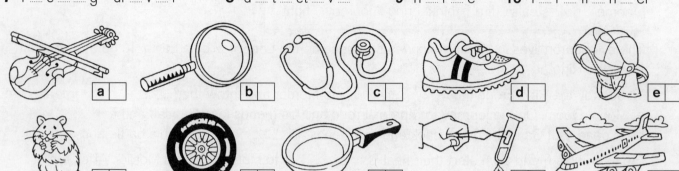

a □   b □   c □   d □   e □

f □   g □   h □   i 1   j □

2 **Match the jobs from Exercise 1 with the descriptions.**

a I have to exercise a lot. I go running every day and I have to keep fit. I have to be very disciplined. 6

e I play in an orchestra. I sometimes play in cafés and restaurants, too. □

b I love science. I work in a laboratory all day. It seems a quiet, routine job – but to me it's really interesting. □

f I do this job because I'm interested in medicine and helping animals. □

c I work in a hospital. I'm always busy! There are lots of things to do and patients to help. □

g I work with a great team. And yes, I love cars and speed! □

d It's a very important job because we save lives. In a fire you have to think very quickly and work as a team. □

h I love solving problems. In my job I have to solve difficult problems to find criminals and stop crime. □

3 **What do you think? Write the jobs next to the adjectives.**

interesting ....   dangerous ....
boring ....   exciting ....

4 **Complete the sentences with the phrases in the box.**

~~'m going to~~   're going to   's going to   isn't going to   aren't going to

I want to be a doctor so I ¹ _'m going to_ study medicine. **Emma**

We don't like horror films. We ² .... watch the horror film on TV tonight. **Naomi**

I've got the plane tickets! We ³ .... have a holiday in Australia! **Ellie**

My sister Phoebe ⁴ .... see her friends this evening. She's worried about her exams. **Kyle**

My cousin's got a new DV cam. She ⁵ .... make a film! **Dylan**

be going to

1 Look at the pictures and complete the sentences with *going to* and these phrases.

> go on the internet   win the race   have pizza   study   watch TV   ~~play tennis~~

1 Joe's
<u>going to play tennis</u>
after school.

4 Hannah ....
....
tomorrow.

2 Luca and Felix ....
....
next Saturday.

5 I ....
this afternoon.

3 We ....
at the weekend.

6 They ....
....
tonight.

2 Write about Alex and Jenny's plans for next year.

NEXT YEAR!	
Alex	**Jenny**
read more books	act in a play
remember my homework!	write a blog
learn Spanish	learn Spanish
do more sport	do more sport

1 Alex is going to read more books.
2 Jenny ....
3 Alex ....
4 Jenny ....
5 They ....
6 They ....

3 Write about what Sophie does *not* intend to do next year.

1 I'm not going to talk in class.
2 ....
3 ....
4 ....
5 ....
6 ....

NEXT YEAR
talk in class **✗**
go to bed late **✗**
forget Mum's birthday **✗**
eat junk food **✗**
argue with my sister **✗**
watch too much TV **✗**

4 Reorder the words to make questions.

1 you / going / cook / to / are / what / ?
What are you going to cook?

2 I / am / to / going / where / stay / ?

3 meet / they / are / who / going / to / ?

4 much / going / it / how / to / cost / is / ?

5 start / going / when / film / the / is / to / ?

6 we / to / what / do / are / going / ?

7 arrive / is / to / she / going / when / ?

8 buy / new / is / going / CD / the / to / she / ?

5 Write the questions and short answers.

1 you and Jake / visit / London ?
Q *Are you and Jake going to visit London?*
A (✗) *No, we aren't.*

2 you / change / your website ?
Q ....
A (✓) ....

3 Jake / write / new songs ?
Q ....
A (✓) ....

4 you and Ella / play / on TV ?
Q ....
A (✗) ....

5 you / make / a film ?
Q ....
A (✗) ....

6 you and Ella / make / a new record ?
Q ....
A (✓) ....

6 Complete the conversation with the correct form of the verbs in brackets and affirmative (✔) or negative (✗) short answers.

A *Are* you *going to fly* (fly) to the Moon?

B .... (✗) We .... (go) to Mars.

A .... you ....(leave) from Cape Canaveral?

B .... (✓)

A .... you ....(walk) on Mars?

B .... (✓) We .... (walk) for two hours.

A .... you ....(write) a book about the trip?

B .... (✓) It ....(be) a bestseller!

7 Write true sentences for you. Use the verbs in the box.

learn	watch	play	see	study
meet	do	go	eat	make	practise
sleep	get up	read	buy	visit	use
talk	tidy	help	write	drink	speak

This evening ...

✔ I'm going to ....

✔ ....

✗ I'm not going to ....

✗ ....

On Saturday ...

✔ ....

✔ ....

✗ ....

✗ ....

1   Label the pictures. Write the names of the musical instruments.

1 ....   2 ....   3 ....   4 ....

5 ....   6 ....   7 ....   8 ....

2   Circle the correct answer.

1 Which instrument is the biggest?
   a guitar   **b** cello   **c** violin
2 Which instrument is the smallest?
   a drums   **b** piano   **c** guitar

3 Which instrument is the easiest to learn?
   a saxophone   **b** piano   **c** recorder
4 Which instrument is the loudest?
   a keyboard   **b** drums   **c** violin

3   Complete the sentences for you. Use the names of musical instruments from Exercise 1.

Music and me

I play ....

I want to play ....

I like ....

I don't like ....

Chat zone

⊙ 37   Complete the conversations with the expressions. Then listen and check.

| I guess so.   Hang on.   It's going to be a nightmare!   No worries! |

1 Lewis   Can I use your mobile?
   Max   Yeah, of course.
   Lewis   Thanks.
   Max   ....

2 Tyler   What's wrong?
   Jenny   I don't want to go to Nick's party.
   ....

3 Maria   Come on, Emily. We have to leave now!
   Emily   ....
   I can't find my mobile.

4 Mum   Are you going to do your English homework now?
   Ethan   ....

be going to for predictions

1 Match the pictures with the sentences.

1 It's going to rain. ☐ 3 She's going to have an accident. ☐ 5 He's going to fall asleep. ☐ 7 I'm going to win the race. ☐

2 They're going to miss the bus. ☐ 4 The film's going to start. ☐ 6 The plate is going to break. ☐ 8 The plane is going to land. ☐

a  c  e  g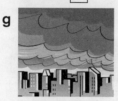

b   d  f  h

2 Look at the pictures and complete the conversations with *going to* and the verbs in the box.

> fail   dance   paint   ~~make~~
> go skateboarding   climb

1 **A** Why is there butter, sugar and flour on the kitchen table?
  B He *'s going to make* a cake!

2 **A** .... Ben .... the exam?
  B Yes, he is. He isn't good at French.

3 **A** Why's Dad wearing those old clothes?
  B He .... the house.

4 **A** What are you going to do?
  B I .... a mountain.

5 **A** Why is Susie wearing that amazing dress?
  B She .... a tango.

6 **A** Why is Antonio carrying a helmet?
  B He .... in the park.

Prepositions of movement – *up, down, into, out of, over, under*

3 Circle with the correct prepostion.

1  2

3  4

5  6

1 Bob is going **under**/down the box.
2 He's going into/up the box.
3 He's climbing up/over the box.
4 He's getting up/out of the box.
5 He's jumping over/under the box.
6 He's falling into/out of the box.

4 Look at the picture and complete the instructions with the prepostions in the box.

> into   out of   over (x2)   in front of
> up (x2)   under   down

Go ¹ ....over.... two hills and
² .... the mountain. Walk
³ .... the mountain and go
⁴ .... the bridge. There is a
tunnel ⁵ .... the bridge. Walk
⁶ .... the tunnel. The tunnel
is ⁷ .... the castle. Take the
treasure out of the box and then
walk ⁸ .... the tunnel. Climb
⁹ .... the castle wall.
Good luck!

Communication

⊙ **38** Complete the conversations. Then listen and check.

> like   what   rain   is   lovely   what's   going   it's

1 Mark Hi Molly. What a ¹ .... day!
Molly Yes, it's really beautiful!

2 Rosie ² .... the weather going to be
³ .... tomorrow?
Hannah It's ⁴ .... to be hot and sunny.

3 Maisie ⁵ .... it going to get colder tonight?
Matt Yes. ⁶ .... going to snow!

4 Olivia ⁷ .... a horrible day!
Tommy Yes. It's going to ⁸ .... this afternoon.
I've got my umbrella!

Reading

1 Read the article and match the paragraphs with the questions.

1 How often is the marathon held?   B
2 How many people take part in the marathon?   ....
3 What's the atmosphere like?   ....
4 How does the race start and finish?   ....
5 What year did the race start?   ....

http://yourspace.cambridge.org

Welcome to the New York City Marathon — the most exciting event ever!

A This is one of the biggest marathons in the world. An incredible 46,795 runners finished the race in 2011!

B Thousands of spectators stand by and cheer the thousands of runners and give them bottles of water as they run past. The 26-mile race is held every year on the first Sunday of November.

C The race started on 13th September, 1970. It became really popular in 1978 when the Norwegian, Grete Waitz, broke the women's world record and ran the 26 miles in an amazing two hours, 32 minutes and 30 seconds. And yes, of course, there was another party at the finish line!

D The marathon runs through all of New York's five boroughs. It starts with a blast from a cannon and shouts from the crowd and ends with cheers and a celebration at the finish line in Central Park.

E It's a crazy event! The atmosphere is unique. It's one big party! Some people wear fancy dress and play drums. Everyone has fun. It's an experience no runner or spectator can ever forget!

2 Read the article again and answer the questions.

1 How many runners finished the race in 2011?   46,795
2 How often is the race held?   ....
3 On what day is the race held?   ....
4 When did the race start?   ....
5 What nationality was Grete Waitz?   ....
6 How many boroughs are there in New York?   ....
7 Where's the finishing line?   ....
8 What instrument do some of the spectators play?   ....

Listening

3 🔘 **39** **Listen and number the sentences in the correct order.**

   a I'm going to sunbathe in the garden. [4]
   b My gran's going to stay with us. ☐
   c My dad's going to buy a car for my sister. ☐

   d I'm going to go to the summer camp. ☐
   e I'm going to stay in bed. ☐

4 🔘 **39** **Listen again and tick (✓) the things Lori, Katie and Ben plan to do this summer.**

	Lori	Katie	Ben
drive to the sea	✓		
play tennis			
walk the dog			
sunbathe			
do homework			
go to the mountains			
stay in bed until 12			
read lots of books			

> **Writing focus**
>
> Check you have used the correct prepositions. Remember:
> *in* + month/year;
> *on* + date;
> *for* + period of time;
> verb *go* + *to*.

Writing

5 **Imagine you are going to run the New York City Marathon. Write an email to a penpal. Say:**

- what you are going to do
- who you are going to travel with
- when you are going to go

- how long you are going to stay in New York
- what you are going to do after the Marathon
- how you feel (excited / nervous?)

Your progress

Look at Student's Book Unit 8. Circle: 😐 = not very well 🙂 = quite well 😎 = very well

I can talk about future intentions.	😐	🙂	😎	p79
I can understand an article about Red Nose Day and find specific information.	😐	🙂	😎	p87
I can listen and understand what people did and are doing for Red Nose Day.	😐	🙂	😎	p87
I can work in a group and make a plan for Red Nose Day.	😐	🙂	😎	p87
I can write an email, about an event in the past and the future.	😐	🙂	😎	p87
I can talk about the weather.	😐	🙂	😎	p115

Your project: my favourite band

- Prepare a presentation about your favourite band. Find information and pictures about:
  Band members their names the instruments they play personal information
  History of the band when and where they started early career biggest achievements
  Discography their most famous albums and songs
  Did you know? interesting facts about the band

- Give your presentation to the class. If possible, include some of their music. Finish with your opinion about the band.
  I think Linkin Park make very interesting music. It's great for dancing.

1 Unscramble the letters and label the planets.

1 hte snu	**5** sram	**8** ausurn
the Sun		
2 eurcrym	**6** turejip	**9** peunent
3 suevn	**7** tarnus	**10** tulop
4 taher		

2 Complete the sentences with the names of planets.

1 We live on .... Earth ....
2 .... is the second planet from the Sun.
3 .... is next to Jupiter and has got rings.
4 .... is next to Jupiter and Earth.
5 .... is between Uranus and Pluto.

3 Describe the positions of the following planets. Write sentences.

1 Mercury ....
....
2 Earth ....
....
3 Jupiter ....
....
4 Pluto ....
....
....

will – positive and negative

1 Look at the map and ⊙circle the correct information in the weather forecast.

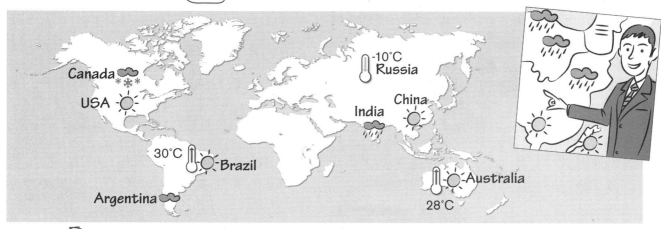

1 It **will** / **won't** be sunny in Brazil.
2 There **will** / **won't** be storms in China.
3 It **will** / **won't** snow in Canada.
4 It **will** / **won't** be cloudy in Argentina.

5 It **will** / **won't** rain in India.
6 There **will** / **won't** be fog in the USA.
7 It **will** / **won't** be cold in Russia.
8 It **will** / **won't** rain in Australia.

2 What will happen to Ruby next week? Look at the pictures and complete the sentences. Use *will* and the verbs in brackets.

1 Ruby .... happy on Monday. (feel)

2 She .... tennis with her friend on Tuesday. (play)

3 Ruby .... busy on Wednesday. (be)

4 On Thursday she .... her dentist. (see)

5 On Friday she .... fun with her best friend. (have)

3 Complete the sentences with *will* or *won't* and the verbs in brackets.

1 Robots ......*will do*...... all the housework. (do)
2 People .... to Jupiter in my lifetime. (not go)
3 I .... a famous writer when I grow up. (be)
4 It .... cold in Moscow in December. (be)
5 They .... the film – it's scary. (not like)
6 I'm tired. I .... well tonight. (sleep)
7 Oscar .... a new car when he gets his first job. (buy)
8 Joel lives too far away. I .... to his party tonight. (not go)

4 Complete the sentences with *will* (✓), *might* (?) or *won't* (✗) and the words in the box.

> win   run   go on holiday   go swimming

1

Larry .... to Mexico. (?)

2

Sara and Lisa .... at the weekend. (✗)

3

Brazil .... the next World Cup. (?)

4

Nicola .... in the London Marathon. (✓)

5 Write predictions for you. Use *will* or *won't* and the words in brackets.

In my life ...

1 (write / a book)
I will write a book.

2 (own / a sports car)
....

3 (be / a pilot)
....

4 (have / a big family)
....

5 (visit / the Moon)
....

6 (climb / a mountain)
....

will – questions and short answers

6 Reorder the words to make questions. Then write answers for you using *will*, *might* or *won't*.

1 play / will / this evening / you / computer games
Will you play computer games this evening?
Yes, I might.

2 your parents / will / tomorrow / go shopping
.............................?
....

3 to school / you / on Saturday / will / go
.............................?
....

4 will / this afternoon / send any text messages / you
.............................?
....

5 on Friday / give you / your English teacher / homework / will
.............................?
....

6 your best friend / at the weekend / you / see / will
.............................?
....

1 For each sentence ⌒circle⌒ two correct answers.

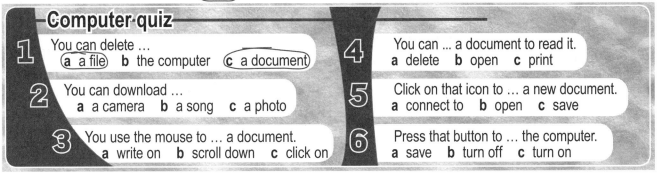

Computer quiz

1 You can delete ...
(a) a file   b the computer   (c) a document

2 You can download ...
a a camera   b a song   c a photo

3 You use the mouse to ... a document.
a write on   b scroll down   c click on

4 You can ... a document to read it.
a delete   b open   c print

5 Click on that icon to ... a new document.
a connect to   b open   c save

6 Press that button to ... the computer.
a save   b turn off   c turn on

2 Complete the cartoons with words from Exercise 1.

A

You have to
2 _____
the computer first,
Mr Jones.

There's something wrong. I can't
1 _connect to_
the internet!

B

Don't 3 _____ on that icon!

Why not?

If you do that, you'll
4 _____
all my photos!

What an amazing story, Emma! Can you
5 _____
down to the bottom of the document? I want to see how it ends.

C

Sure. I can
6 _____
it out for you if you want a copy.

Really? Yes, please!

Chat zone

⊙ **40** Complete the conversations with the expressions. Then listen and check.

| I don't get it.   Come on!   Very clever! |

1 Esme What are you doing?
Jake I'm checking my emails.
Esme _____ We have to leave. The film starts in half an hour!
Jake OK, OK. We'll get there in time.

2 Billy Look at the rain! We'll get really wet.
Sofia Don't worry. I borrowed my mum's umbrella.
Billy _____

3 Lexi Oh no!
Eva What's the problem?
Lexi My mobile won't send text messages.
Eva Can you receive messages?
Lexi Yes, I can. _____ It's really weird.

First conditional

1 Match the sentence halves.

1 They won't go to the cinema
2 I won't go to school tomorrow
3 If she goes to the shops,
4 If we miss the bus,
5 If I don't tidy my room,
6 If you don't take an umbrella,

a you'll get very wet!
b my mum will be annoyed.
c we'll arrive really late.
d if the film ends very late.
e if I don't feel better.
f she'll buy some clothes.

2 Complete the email. Circle the correct answers.

To: Luke
From: Marko

Hi Luke

How are you? What are you doing this summer? Let me tell you about my plans. You know I've got important exams this year. Well, if I **¹ pass / 'll pass** them I **² go / 'll go** to the USA! I want to stay at a summer camp. It will be great fun!

After summer camp, I might visit my aunt and uncle. They've got a big house in the countryside in Texas. They have lots of horses, too! If I **³ spend / will spend** some time with them, they **⁴ take / 'll take** me to visit lots of places – Dallas, New Orleans and maybe Mexico! And maybe I'll go on a boat trip on the Mississippi River. Cool!

If I **⁵ don't pass / won't pass** my exams, I **⁶ go / 'll go** with my family to the seaside. That's not bad really, because if I **⁷ go / 'll go** to Texas, I **⁸ miss / 'll miss** the seaside!

Take care
Marko

3 Read the email in Exercise 2 again. Are the sentences true (T), false (F) or not sure (NS)?

1 Marko will go to the USA this summer. ☐
2 He wants to go to a summer camp. ☐
3 Marko has got relatives in Texas. ☐
4 His uncle and aunt live in Dallas. ☐
5 Marko will go on a boat trip on the Mississippi River. ☐
6 If he passes his exams, Marko will go to the seaside. ☐

4 Complete the sentences with the correct form of the verbs in brackets. Then match four sentences with the pictures.

a   b
c   d

1 If I ___don't finish___ my homework, my teacher ___will be___ annoyed. (not finish / be) [c]
2 We ___ to the concert if we ___ tickets. (go / get)
3 If Alex ___ his pocket money, he ___ a new skateboard. (save / buy) ☐
4 They ___ a picnic on Saturday if the weather ___ nice. (have / be) ☐
5 If you ___ me your phone number, I ___ you a text message. (give / send)
6 If that dog ___ barking, I ___ any sleep tonight! (not stop / not get) ☐

First conditional questions

5 Write the questions and short answers.

1 you watch a DVD / you stay at home this evening (✓)
Will you watch a DVD if you stay at home this evening?
Yes, we will.

2 Isabella study science / she go to university (✓)

....

....

3 they visit Manchester / they go to the UK (✗)

....

....

4 the teacher be angry / we not do our homework (✓)

....

....

5 your friends come to my party / I invite them (✗)

....

....

6 Answer the questions for you.

1 What will you do if your friend invites you to a party tomorrow night?

....

....

2 What will you do if it is cold and wet all weekend?

....

....

3 What will you do if you don't like your dinner tonight?

....

....

4 What will you do if your teacher gives you a lot of homework?

....

....

5 What will you do if it is sunny and warm at the weekend?

....

....

Communication

41 Complete the conversation with the words in the box. Then listen and check.

idea	sure	don't	true	all	agree	what

Tom OK, let's do the 'True or False' quiz. What's question one?

Katie 'Mars is the fifth planet from the Sun.' I think it's ¹........................ .

Tom Are you ²........................ ?

Katie Erm ... well, Mercury is the first planet from the Sun, Venus is the second. Earth is the third and Jupiter is the fourth. I think Mars is the fifth.

Grace I ³........................ agree. I'm sure Mars is the fourth planet, and Jupiter is the fifth planet from the Sun.

Tom ⁴........................ do you think, George?

George I've got no ⁵........................ !

Tom Well, I ⁶........................ with Grace.

Katie Me too. Do we ⁷........................ agree?

George Yes, OK. Mars isn't the fifth planet from the Sun. Let's write 'False'.

Reading

1 Read the article and match the headings with the paragraphs.

a How is Mars similar to Earth? **d** So how will people live?

b Why will humans live on other planets? **e** Will we be able to live on Mars?

c Would you like to live on Mars? **f** Why do you think they will live on Mars?

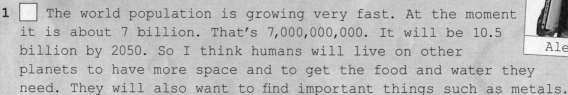

This week we interview Alex Newton. Alex is an astronomer and scientist. And he believes there will be a human base on Mars before the end of the century.

Alex Newton

1 ☐ The world population is growing very fast. At the moment it is about 7 billion. That's 7,000,000,000. It will be 10.5 billion by 2050. So I think humans will live on other planets to have more space and to get the food and water they need. They will also want to find important things such as metals.

2 ☐ First of all, it is the closest planet to Earth. Secondly, it is the planet most similar to Earth in the solar system.

3 ☐a Mars has seasons like summer and winter. It also has clouds. And we think it has water, too. A day on Mars is only 37 minutes longer than a day on Earth. But a year takes 687 days!

4 ☐ Yes, we will. However, we won't be able to breathe on the planet. There isn't enough oxygen. And it's also very cold. The average temperature is –63°C! So people will wear space suits when they go outside their special buildings.

5 ☐ People will live under large domes. In these buildings, people will grow all the food they need. They will go outside to get important metals such as iron and aluminium.

6 ☐ Yes, I would. I think it will be a great adventure. I'm only 35 now, so I hope it will happen in my life!

A future human base on Mars

2 Read the article again. Are the sentences true (*T*) or false (*F*)? Correct the false information.

1 The world population is about six billion. ☐F *It's about seven billion.*

2 Alex thinks people will go into space because there won't be enough food and water on Earth. ☐

3 Mars is the planet nearest the Earth. ☐

4 A day on Mars is shorter than a day on Earth. ☐

5 A year on Mars is longer than a year on Earth. ☐

6 It is much colder on Mars than on Earth. ☐

7 People will have to live in special buildings on Mars. ☐

8 People will get the food they need from Earth. ☐

Listening

3 ⊙ **42** **Listen and complete the fact file.**

FACTFILE

Name	Lauren Brook
Job	....
Age	....
Ambition	To travel to ....

4 ⊙ **42** **Listen again and ⊙circle the correct information.**

1 Lauren went on a space walk last **month** / **year.**
2 Lauren's space walk was the **best** / **worst** experience of her life.
3 The last time people were on the Moon was on **13th** / **30th** December 1972.
4 Lauren is **certain** / **uncertain** that people will walk on the Moon again.
5 Lauren thinks people are **better** / **worse** than robots in space.
6 She thinks that **Venus** / **Mars** will be the first planet people travel to.

Writing

5 **Imagine it is the year 2100 and you are a teenager living on Mars. Write a message to your penpal on Earth. Talk about:**

- where you live and what it is like.
- the things you do in a normal day.
- what you want to do after you leave school.

> **Writing focus**
>
> Check you have used the correct tenses. Remember: we use the present simple to talk about facts and routines.

Your progress

Look at Student's Book Unit 9. Circle: ☹ = not very well ☺ = quite well 😎 = very well

I can make predictions about the future and talk about possible events.	☹ ☺ 😎	p89 p94
I can plan a website with my partner and talk about technology.	☹ ☺ 😎	p93
I can read and understand an article about robots and find specific information.	☹ ☺ 😎	p97
I can listen to a TV programme and understand the main points.	☹ ☺ 😎	p97
I can write a paragraph about my life, my family and my possessions.	☹ ☺ 😎	p97
I can work in a team, showing I am certain or uncertain or checking others' opinions.	☹ ☺ 😎	p116

Your project: space station

- Design a space station. Think of a name and draw a plan.
- Label the different areas of the space station (e.g. gym, laboratories, cinema, control room, sleeping area).
- Write a description of what happens in each area.
- Make a poster about your space station. Include drawings and photos.
- Put up the space station posters on the classroom wall. Choose: the funniest   the most creative   the biggest   the smallest   the strangest

1 Look at the pictures and match the verbs with the nouns.

1	play	**a**	a cricket match
2	swim	**b**	skiing
3	meet	**c**	a trophy
4	win	**d**	a sports star
5	score	**e**	a goal
6	go	**f**	a horse
7	watch	**g**	100 metres
8	run	**h**	badminton
9	ride	**i**	a marathon

2 Unscramble the words and write the past participles. Then match them with the verbs in Exercise 1.

a delapy — played 1
b nego — .... ☐
c urn — .... ☐
d techwad — .... ☐
e tem — .... ☐
f recods — .... ☐
g smuw — .... ☐
h now — .... ☐
i dedrin — .... ☐

3 Write six true sentences for you using the verbs in Exercise 2.

I have ...
ridden a bike.

I haven't ...
met a sports star.

Chat zone

43 Complete the conversations with the expressions. Then listen and check.

> What a shame!   It was a laugh.   Go on then.

1 Tom Let's go swimming.
Jim I'm not sure. The water looks a bit cold. You go first.
Tom OK.
Jim ....
Tom All right, I will!

2 Suzy Did you go to the beach yesterday?
Jim Yes, I did. ....

Suzy Why?
Jim Tom wanted to go swimming. But the water was freezing!
Suzy Did you go swimming, too?
Jim No way!

3 Jim Do you want to play football?
Tom I'm sorry, but I can't.
Jim What's the problem?
Tom I don't feel well. I've got a horrible cold.
Jim ....

Present perfect – positive and negative statements

1 Circle the ten regular past participles in the word snake.

studied carried planned travelled played lived started opened married dropped

2 Complete the messages. Use past participles from Exercise 1.

> **What are your most amazing experiences? And what about your friends and family? Let me know!**

1 My dad .... in seven countries! *superboy*

2 I .... in a football match at Wembley. *footballmad*

3 We .... around Europe in a camper van. *banana*

4 My uncle is amazing. He .... more than three hundred people. He's a priest! Hahahaha! *fluffy*

3 Match the words to make activities.

1 climb **2** read **3** play **4** act
5 write **6** visit **7** dive **8** carry

a the piano **b** a heavy suitcase
c into the sea **d** an ancient city
e a book in English **f** in a play
g a tree **h** a poem

4 Write positive and negative sentences for you. Use the activities in Exercise 3.

1 I haven't climbed a mountain.
2 ....
3 ....
4 ....
5 ....
6 ....
7 ....
8 ....

5 Complete the sentences for you.

All about me!

1 The best film / see
The best film I've ever seen is Avatar.

2 The worst food / eat

3 The most beautiful place / visit

4 The best book / read

5 The most boring game / play

6 The most exciting thing / do

Questions with *Have you ever?*

6 Match the questions with the short answers.

1 Has your granddad ever listened to hip-hop?

2 Have you ever written a poem?

3 Has your sister ever performed on stage?

4 Have you and Carmen ever had a pet?

5 Have your parents watched this DVD?

6 Have I spent all my pocket money?

a No, she hasn't.

b Yes, you have.

c Yes, he has!

d No, they haven't.

e Yes, we have.

f No, I haven't.

8 Complete the conversation. Use the information from Exercise 7.

Charlie Hey, Imogen! Can I ask you some questions? It's for a school project.

Imogen Sure. I hope they aren't difficult.

Charlie No, they're easy questions!
Have you ever been to a concert?

Imogen Yes, I have.

Charlie ....

Imogen ....

Charlie ....

Imogen ....

Charlie ....

Imogen ....

Charlie ....

Imogen ....

Charlie ....

Imogen ....

Charlie Thanks, Imogen. That was great!

7 Match the activities with the pictures.

In my life ...	
1 go to a concert	✓
2 do karate	✗
3 juggle	✓
4 go to an art gallery	✗
5 have an accident	✓
6 be late for school	✗

Imogen

a

c

d

b

e

f

1 🔘 **44** Read the quiz and (circle) the correct answers. Then listen and check.

The Your Space Quiz

What do you remember?
Do the quiz and find out.

1 **Which planet is nearest to the Sun?**

a Mars
b Mercury
c Venus

2 **Where was the 2010 Football World Cup?**

a China
b South Africa
c France

3 **What does this emoticon mean?**

a surprised
b embarrassed
c angry

4 **During a thunderstorm, you have to ...**

a stand under tall trees.
b put up your umbrella.
c stay away from tall trees.

5 **How long did the oldest recorded elephant live?**

a 36 years
b 82 years
c 101 years

6 **If you go to Trafalgar Square in London, you will see ...**

a Big Ben.
b The London Eye.
c Nelson's Column.

7 **Every year Americans throw away 30 per cent of the world's rubbish. That is ...**

a too much.
b too many.
c not enough.

8 **Which famous character did Mark Twain create?**

a Long John Silver
b Huckleberry Finn
c Sherlock Holmes

9 **How many colours are there on the Brazilian flag?**

a two
b three
c four

10 **On 17 June 1928, Amelia Earhart ...**

a was water-skiing across the Atlantic Ocean.
b was swimming across the Atlantic Ocean.
c was flying across the Atlantic Ocean.

11 **You .... reply to text messages from strangers.**

a should
b shouldn't
c don't have to

12 **What is going to happen next? James is going to .... the cat.**

a catch
b drop
c run away from

Making comparisons

1 Complete the sentences with comparative adjectives and *than*. Use the adjectives in the box.

> expensive heavy ~~fast~~ dangerous
> cheap long noisy tall

1 A train is faster than a bicycle.
2 The Amazon River .... the Mississippi River.
3 Text messages .... phone calls.
4 A painting by Picasso .... a poster.
5 The Eiffel Tower .... the London Eye.
6 Elephants .... giraffes.
7 An electric guitar .... a violin.
8 Mountain climbing .... walking.

Talking about the past

3 Complete the next episode of the story of Donna and Richard. Put the verbs in brackets in the correct form.

2 Write sentences about your family. Use the superlative form of the adjectives in the box.

> funny intelligent old
> tall young ~~interesting~~

1 My uncle Carlos is the most interesting. He's an artist!
2 ....
....
3 ....
....
4 ....
....
5 ....
....
6 ....
....

The story so far.

Donna and Richard were walking along a beach when they heard a strange noise. Then they saw a hole form in the sand ... and they fell into it!
Now read on.
Donna and Richard ¹ hit (hit) the ground with a loud bump.
'Are you OK?' asked Richard.
'I think so,' said Donna.
They ² .... (look) up. Light ³ .... (shine) into the hole. Then they looked around them. Donna and Richard couldn't believe their eyes. They ⁴ .... (stand) next to the entrance to a tunnel!
'That is so strange!' said Donna. 'Where do you think the tunnel goes?'
'I don't know,' said Richard. 'Let's find out.'
They ⁵ .... (walk) along the tunnel when

Richard said, 'Stop!'
'What ⁶ .... (hear)?' asked Donna.
'Nothing,' said Richard. 'But take a look at this.'
Donna couldn't see anything at first. But while she ⁷ .... (look), she ⁸ .... (notice) a pattern of straight lines.
'Hey, it's a map!' she said.
'That's right,' said a man behind them.
They quickly ⁹ .... (turn) round and saw a tall man. He ¹⁰ .... (wear) a uniform and he ¹¹ .... (not seem) very happy. He was a security officer.
'How did you get here?' he asked.
'We fell down a hole,' explained Richard.
'And then we ¹² .... (walk) down this tunnel,' said Donna.
'I don't believe you,' said the man. 'Come with me.'

Talking about the present

4 Complete the questions and write answers for you.

1 Your friend What ___are you doing___ (do) at the moment?

You ___

2 Your friend What ___ (wear)?

You ___

3 Your friend How much TV ___ (watch) every day?

You ___

4 Your friend What time ___ (usually, get up)?

You ___

5 Your friend ___ (listen) to any music at the moment?

You ___

6 Your friend How often ___ (tidy) your room?

You ___

Giving advice

5 Match the problems with the advice. Then complete the advice with *should* or *shouldn't*.

1 I'm thirsty. 〔g〕
2 My brother's angry with me. □
3 Should I eat sweets every day? □
4 I can't remember new words in English. □
5 The teacher is annoyed with Nick. □
6 I don't understand this word. □
7 My dog isn't very well. □
8 Ouch! My face is red. □

a You ___ use his computer.
b You ___ keep a vocabulary notebook.
c He ___ talk in the lesson.
d You ___ use a dictionary.
e You ___ take it to the vet.
f You ___ sit in the sun.
g You ___should___ have a drink.
h No, you ___ .

Communication

Making compliments

1 ◉ **45** Put the sentences in the correct order. Then listen and check.

□ Thanks, Amelia.
□ Hi, Ethan. Hey, I love your T-shirt!
□ Happy birthday, Ethan!
□ A present?
〔1〕 Hi, Amelia.
□ Yeah. My birthday was on Saturday.
□ Thanks. It was a present.

2 ◉ **46** Complete the conversations with the words in the box. Then listen and check.

| love mine what new cool think thanks cap |

1 Ben Your skateboard is really [1] ___ .
Mike Thanks. It's [2] ___ .

2 Lea I like your [3] ___ .
Sam Thanks. But it isn't [4] ___ . It's my brother's!

3 Tom I [5] ___ your trainers.
Ellie [6] ___ . I got them last week.

4 Sara [7] ___ a fantastic bag!
Dani Do you [8] ___ so? Thanks!

Reading

1 Read the article and match the people with the activities.

1	Spider-Man	**a**	saved the lives of lots of people.
2	David Beckham	**b**	helps poor children in Colombia.
3	Florence Nightingale	**c**	fights crime.
4	Leon's neighbour	**d**	started a charity that gives wheelchairs to children.
5	Shakira	**e**	does small jobs for people.

What is a hero?
by Leon Jackson

What do you think of when you see the word 'hero'? Do you think of superheroes such as Spider-Man or Superman? Or perhaps you think of famous people from the past like Florence Nightingale or Princess Diana. A hero usually helps people. Or he or she does something good for a community. For example, Spider-Man fights crime. And Florence Nightingale saved the lives of lots of people in hospitals in the nineteenth century.

Unfortunately, for lots of people today, their heroes are celebrities. These celebrities are famous because they are film stars or pop stars, or just because they are beautiful and appear on TV! In my opinion, they aren't real heroes. But some celebrities can be heroes and good role models. For example, David Beckham is a famous footballer and Shakira is a singer. But they both do work for UNICEF, an international charity that helps children. Beckham also started a charity that gives wheelchairs to children. Shakira started a charity that provides special schools for poor children in Colombia. Their work improves the lives of many children all over the world.

Heroes can be young or old. And they can come from any country. They can do important things to improve the lives of thousands of people. Or they can do small things that help only a few people.

My hero is my neighbour. He's a postman. I know that doesn't sound very exciting. But my neighbour knows all the old people in the neighbourhood. He checks they are OK. Sometimes he does their shopping for them. He isn't famous but he makes a big difference to their lives.

So who is your hero? Let me know!

2 Read the article again and (circle) the best answers.

1 In Leon's opinion, a hero is a person who ...
  a is famous.
  b does something good for people.

2 For many people today, their heroes are ...
  a celebrities.
  b people from history.

3 David Beckham and Shakira are real heroes because ...
  a they improve the lives of many people.
  b they are famous all over the world.

4 Leon believes that ...
  a all famous people are heroes.
  b heroes can be normal people like you or me.

Listening

3 ○ 47 **Alex is giving a talk about his hero to the class. Listen and complete the information.**

1 Einstein was born in 1879 in ......Germany...... .
2 He left college in ....
3 He wrote his theory of relativity when he was .... years old.
4 He won the Nobel Prize for physics in ....
5 He became a professor at Princeton University in ....
6 Einstein died on ....

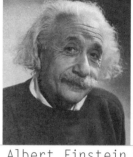

Albert Einstein

4 ○ 47 **Listen again and complete the sentences.**

1 Alex thinks the theory of relativity was the most .... scientific idea of the twentieth century.
2 Einstein is his role model because he had .... ideas.
3 Alex thinks we must have .... to make the world a better place.

Writing

5 **Write a short biography about your hero or role model. Include some interesting facts.**

- **paragraph 1**   birth and early life
- **paragraph 2**   education and later life
- **paragraph 3**   the reason he/she is/was famous
- **paragraph 4**   the reason he/she is your hero

> **Writing focus**
>
> When you have finished writing, check your work carefully:
> - Is the spelling correct?
> - Is the punctuation correct?
> - Is the grammar correct? Pay attention to tenses, prepositions and articles.

Your progress

Look at Student's Book Unit 10. Circle: ☹ = not very well ☺ = quite well 😎 = very well

I can talk about my experiences.	☹ ☺ 😎	p101
I can use language relating to the present, past and future.	☹ ☺ 😎	pp102–104
I can read and understand an article about Lewis Hamilton's life.	☹ ☺ 😎	p106
I can listen to and understand key information about Shanaze Reade's life.	☹ ☺ 😎	p107
I can write a biography of a sports star, dividing it into three paragraphs.	☹ ☺ 😎	p107
I can make and accept compliments.	☹ ☺ 😎	p117

Your project: my favourite sport

- Prepare a computer presentation or poster about your favourite sport.
- Find information and pictures from the internet or books. Include:
  - when and where it started
  - how many people do it
  - the equipment you need
  - the most famous teams or sports personalities
  - why you like it
- Give your presentation to the class.

Present simple

Unit 1

Positive		Negative			Questions			Short answers					
I You We They	play.	I You We They	do not don't		Do	you we they	play?	Yes,	I you we they	do.	No,	I you we they	don't.
				play.		I			I			I	
He She It	plays.	He She It	does not doesn't		Does	he she it			he she it	does.		he she it	doesn't.

We use the present simple to talk about regular activities, routines and facts:
*I **watch** TV after school. They **don't wear** jeans every day. Do you **go** to the same school? Yes, we **do**.*
The spelling of the verb changes in the third person singular. Add an **-s** to the verb:
*She play**s** basketball after school.*
Add **-es** to verbs ending in **-ch**, **-o**, **-sh**, **-s**, **-ss**, **-x**, **-z**: *watch* ⟶ *watch**es**, go* ⟶ *go**es***
Add **-ies** to verbs ending in **-y** after a consonant: *try* ⟶ *tr**ies***

Countable / uncountable

Unit 1

Countable nouns have singular and plural forms: *book – books, photo – photos*
Uncountable nouns don't have plural forms because we can't count them: *food, money*
We use **some** with plural countable nouns and with uncountable nouns to talk about quantity:
some *sweets,* **some** *ice cream*
We use **some** in positive sentences and we use **any** in negative sentences and questions:
*I've got **some** photos.   There aren't **any** games.   Is there **any** information?*

too much / too many

Unit 1

We use **too much** with uncountable nouns: **too much** *time,* **too much** *paper*
We use **too many** with countable nouns: **too many** *books,* **too many** *ideas*

Present continuous

Unit 1

Positive			Negative			Questions			Short answers					
I	am 'm		I	am not 'm not		Am	I		I	am.		I	am not. 'm not.
He She It	is 's	reading.	He She It	is not isn't	reading.	Is	he she it	reading?	Yes,	he she it	is.	No,	he she it	is not. isn't.
We You They	are 're		We You They	are not aren't		Are	we you they			we you they	are.		we you they	are not. aren't.

We use the present continuous to talk about actions that are happening at the time of speaking:
*I'm **sitting** on the sofa. Tom **isn't reading**. **Are** they **dancing**? Yes, they **are**.*

Present simple / present continuous Unit 1

We use the present simple to talk about routines and regular activities. We usually use adverbs of frequency: *always, usually, often, sometimes, never.*

We use the present continuous to talk about actions happening now. We usually use these time expressions: *now, at the moment, today.*

*We usually **go** shopping on Saturdays. Today we**'re going** to the cinema.*

can Unit 1

Positive and negative			Questions			Short answers					
I				I			I			I	
He She It	can can't	draw.	Can	he she it	draw?	Yes,	he she it	can.	No,	he she it	can't.
We You They				we you they			we you they			we you they	

We use **can** to talk about abilities. It has the same form for all persons. It is followed by the verb without to:

*I **can** juggle.*

*She **can't** dance.*

***Can** they skateboard? Yes, they **can**.*

Past simple – *be* Unit 2

Positive		Negative		Questions		Short answers					
I he she it	was	I he she it	was not wasn't	Was	I ... ? he ... ? she ... ? it ... ?	Yes,	I he she it	was.	No,	I he she it	wasn't.
we you they	were	we you they	were not weren't	Were	we ... ? you ... ? they ... ?	Yes,	we you they	were.	No,	we you they	weren't.

We use **was/were** to talk about situations in the past. We use **was** with *I / he / she / it* and **were** with *you / we / they* :

*I **was** late for school.*

*They **weren't** very noisy.*

***Were** you in the cinema? Yes, we **were**.*

there was / there were Unit 2

Positive	Negative	Questions	Short answers
There was a birthday cake.	There wasn't any music.	Was there a big cake?	Yes, there was. No, there wasn't.
There were lots of sandwiches.	There weren't any crisps.	Were there lots of people?	Yes, there were. No, there weren't.

Past simple – regular verbs

Units 2 and 3

Positive		Negative			Questions				Short answers						
I		I				I				I				I	
He She It	started. studied. stopped.	He She It	did not didn't	start. study. stop.	Did	he she it	start? study? stop?	Yes,	he she it	did.	No,	he she it	didn't
We You They		We You They				we you they				we you they				we you they	

We use the past simple to talk about finished situations or actions in the past.
We use the same form for all persons:
I arrived late. They walked in the countryside.
We form negatives and questions with *did* + verb:
They didn't arrive. Did you text me? Yes, I did.
Add **-ed** to make the past simple of most verbs: *cook* ⟶ *cooked, watch* ⟶ *watched*
Add **-d** to verbs ending in **-e**: *decide* ⟶ *decided, live* ⟶ *lived*
With verbs ending in **-y** after a consonant, change **-y** to **-i** and add **-ed**: *try* ⟶ *tried*
With 1-syllable verbs ending in vowel + consonant, double the consonant and add **-ed**: *stop* ⟶ *stopped*

Past simple – irregular verbs

Units 2 and 3

Many verbs are irregular and do not add *-ed* to the verb to form the past simple positive form:
Mum gave me a new bike. Josh won a prize. I lost my mobile phone in the park.
See page 91 for a list of irregular verbs.

could

Unit 3

Positive and negative			Questions				Short answers						
I				I				I				I	
He She It	could couldn't	swim.	Could	he she it	swim?	Yes,	he she it	could.	No,	he she it	couldn't.
We You They				we you they				we you they				we you they	

Could is the past form of *can*. We use *could* + verb to talk about the things we were able to do at specific times in the past:
When I was four, I could play the piano. I couldn't play the guitar.

as … as / not as … as

Unit 4

We use *as* + adjective + *as* to say that two things are the same:
Paul is as tall as Mike.
We use *not as* + adjective + *as* to say that two things are not the same:
The Amazon is not as long as the Nile.

Comparative and superlative adjectives

Unit 4

adjective	comparative	superlative
long	longer	the longest
clean	cleaner	the cleanest
large	larger	the largest
big	bigger	the biggest
heavy	heavier	the heaviest
boring	more boring	the most boring

We use comparative adjectives + *than* to compare two things:
*Winter is **colder than** summer. New York is **more exciting than** London.*
We use superlative adjectives to describe one thing in a group of three or more:
*I'm **the smallest** boy in the class.*

Spelling rules
Adjectives with 1 syllable, add **-er/-est**: *long* ⟶ *long**er*** ⟶ *long**est***
Adjectives ending **-e**: add **-r/-st**: *large* ⟶ *larg**er*** ⟶ *larg**est***
Adjectives ending vowel + consonant, double the consonant and add **-er/-est**:
big ⟶ *big**ger*** ⟶ *big**gest***
Adjectives ending **-y**, change the **-y** to **-i** and add **-er/-est**: *dry* ⟶ *drier* ⟶ *driest*
Adjectives with 2 or more syllables, use **more** and **most**: *boring* ⟶ **more** *boring* ⟶ **the most** *boring,*
expensive ⟶ **more** *expensive* ⟶ **the most** *expensive*
Some adjectives do not follow the rules: *good* ⟶ **better** ⟶ **the best**, *bad* ⟶ **worse** ⟶ **the worst**,
far ⟶ **further** ⟶ **the furthest**

Future arrangements

Unit 5

We use the present continuous to talk about fixed plans and arrangements in the future:
*I'**m going** to Greece next week. She'**s flying** to Paris on Monday. What **are** you **doing** tomorrow?*
We use **would like to** to invite someone to do something:
***Would** you **like to** come to the cinema tonight? Yes, I **would**. / No, I **wouldn't**.*

Talking about future plans

Unit 5

We use the present continuous when we are sure about our plans:
*I'**m meeting** Ed this afternoon.*
We use **may/might** when we are not sure about our plans:
*What are you doing this evening? I don't know. I **may/might** watch a film.*

must

Unit 6

Positive	I / You / He / She / It / We / You / They	must	put plastic cups in the recycling bin.
Negative	I / You / He / She / It / We / You / They	mustn't	use a mobile phone in the canteen.

We use **must** + verb to talk about rules and personal obligation:
*You **must** be quiet in the library.*
We use **mustn't** + verb to say that something is prohibited:
*We **mustn't** use our mobile phones at school.*

have to

Unit 6

Positive			Negative			Questions				Short answers		
I You We They	have to		I You We They	don't have to		Do	I you we they	have to	go?	Yes,	I / you / we / they	do.
		go.			go.						he / she / it	does.
He She It	has to		He She It	doesn't have to		Does	he she it			No,	I / you / we / they	don't.
											he / she / it	doesn't.

We use **have to** + verb to talk about an obligation from someone else: *I **have to** see the dentist.*

We use **don't have to** + verb when there is no obligation: *We **don't have to** go to school tomorrow.*

should

Unit 6

Positive and negative			Questions			Short answers					
I He She It	should shouldn't	run.	Should	I he she it we you they	run?	Yes,	I he she it we you they	should.	No,	I he she it we you they	shouldn't.
We You They											

We use **should** + verb to give advice and suggestions:

*I feel really unfit. You **should** do some sport.*

*I haven't got any money. You **shouldn't** buy so many clothes.*

Imperative

Unit 6

We use imperatives to give advice, warnings, instructions and orders.

We form the imperative with the base form of the verb without the subject: ***Check*** *your spelling.*

We form the negative with *don't* + base form of the verb: ***Don't*** *use capital letters.*

Past continuous

Unit 7

Positive			Negative			Questions			Short answers		
I He She It	was	working writing chatting	I He She It	was not wasn't	working writing chatting	Was	I he she it	working? writing? chatting?	Yes,	I / he / she / it	was.
We You They	were		We You They	were not weren't		Were	we you they			we / you / they	were.
									No,	I / he / she / it	wasn't.
										we / you / they	weren't.

We use the past continuous to talk about actions that were in progress at a particular time in the past.

The form is **was/were** + verb + **-ing**:

*At one o'clock I **was having** lunch. I **wasn't playing** computer games.*

Were *they **watching** TV yesterday at ten o'clock? Yes, they **were**.*

Past simple v. past continuous
Unit 7

Past continuous ↓ **Past simple**

*Kim **was flying** a kite when he **saw** the eagle.*

We use the past continuous to talk about an action that was in progress at a particular time in the past (*Kim **was flying** a kite*).

We use the past simple to talk about another action that interrupted it (when *he **saw** the eagle*).

be going to
Unit 8

Positive			Negative			Questions			Short answers					
I	am 'm		I	am not 'm not		Am	I			I	am.		I	'm not.
He She It	is 's	**going to** go.	He She It	is not isn't	**going to** go.	Is	he she it	**going to** go?	Yes,	he she it	is.	No,	he she it	isn't.
We You They	are 're		We You They	are not aren't		Are	we you they			we you they	are.		we you they	aren't.

We use **be going to** + verb to talk about something we intend to do in the future:
*I**'m going to** study Maths at university.* ***Is** she **going to** be a vet? No, she **isn't**.*
We also use *be going to* for predictions based on something we can see in the present:
*Look at those clouds! It**'s going to** rain.*

will
Unit 9

Positive			Negative			Questions			Short answers					
I			I				I			I			I	
He She It	will 'll	go.	He She It	will not won't	go.	Will	he she it	go?	Yes,	he she it	will.	No,	he she it	won't.
We You They			We You They				we you they			we you they			we you they	

We use **will** + verb without *to* to make predictions about the future. It has the same form for all persons:
*I **will** live in Paris.* *They **won't** get married.* ***Will** he learn to drive? Yes, he **will**.*
We often use *think* when we make predictions:
*I **think** I**'ll** go to university.*

First conditional
Unit 9

Condition: *if* + present simple				Result: *will/won't* + verb			
If	I / we / you / they	go	to Paris,	I / we / you / they	will		visit the Louvre.
	he / she / it	goes	to Paris,	he / she / it	won't		

Questions							Short answers		
Will	I / we / you / they	play tennis	if	I / we / you / they	go	to the park?	Yes,	I / we / you / they he / she / it	will.
	he / she / it			he / she / it	goes		No,	I / we / you / they he / she / it	won't.

We use the first conditional to talk about possible future events and their results.

We use the present simple for the condition and *will/won't* + verb for the result:

If I'm late, I'll call you on my mobile.

The condition can come before or after the result. Use a comma if the condition comes first:

If you're hungry, I'll buy some chocolate.   *I'll buy some chocolate if you're hungry.*

We put question words before the result:

***What** will you drink if you're thirsty?* ***Where** will they go if they have a holiday?*

Present perfect
Unit 10

Positive				Negative				Questions				Short answers		
I We You They	have 've		worked.	I We You They	have not haven't		worked.	Have	I we you they		worked?	Yes,	I / we / you / they	have.
													he / she / it	has.
He She It	has 's			He She It	has not hasn't			Has	he she it			No,	I / we / you / they	haven't.
													he / she / it	hasn't.

We use the present perfect to talk about past actions and events in a time period up to the present:

I've climbed mountains in Switzerland.

⟵──────────────────⟶

past   **now**

The form is ***have/has*** + past participle of the verb: *I've visited New York. She's acted in a play.*

The past participles of regular verbs end in **-d** or **-ed** and have the same form as the past simple. See page 91 for a list of irregular verbs.

We form negatives with ***have/has not*** + past participle:

*I **haven't flown** in a plane. He **hasn't read** this book.*

The word order in questions is: ***Have/Has*** + subject + past participle. We don't repeat the past participle in short answers:

***Has** Julia **had** lunch? Yes, she **has**. / No, she **hasn't**.*

The present perfect is often used with *ever* to ask about life experience: ***Have** you **ever been** to China?*

Irregular verbs

Verb	Past simple	Past participle
be	was/were	been
beat	beat	beaten
become	became	become
begin	began	begun
bite	bit	bitten
break	broke	broken
bring	brought	brought
build	built	built
buy	bought	bought
catch	caught	caught
choose	chose	chosen
come	came	come
cost	cost	cost
cut	cut	cut
do	did	done
drink	drank	drunk
drive	drove	driven
eat	ate	eaten
fall	fell	fallen
feel	felt	felt
fight	fought	fought
find	found	found
fly	flew	flown
forget	forgot	forgotten
get	got	got
give	gave	given
go	went	gone
grow	grew	grown
hang	hung	hung
have	had	had
hear	heard	heard
hit	hit	hit
hold	held	held
keep	kept	kept
know	knew	known

Verb	Past simple	Past participle
leave	left	left
lose	lost	lost
make	made	made
meet	met	met
pay	paid	paid
put	put	put
read	read	read
ride	rode	ridden
ring	rang	rung
run	ran	run
say	said	said
see	saw	seen
sell	sold	sold
send	sent	sent
shake	shook	shaken
sing	sang	sung
sink	sank	sunk
sit	sat	sat
sleep	slept	slept
speak	spoke	spoken
spend	spent	spent
stand	stood	stood
steal	stole	stolen
swim	swam	swum
take	took	taken
teach	taught	taught
tell	told	told
think	thought	thought
understand	understood	understood
upset	upset	upset
wake	woke	woken
wear	wore	worn
win	won	won
write	wrote	written

(n) = noun   (v) = verb
(adj) = adjective
(adv) = adverb
(excl) = exclamation
(exp) = expression

Unit 1

alarm clock (n) /ə'lɑːm ˌklɒk/
also (adv) /'ɔːl.səʊ/
always (adv) /'ɔːl.weɪz/
appearance (n) /ə'pɪə.rəns/
Arabic (n) /'ær.ə.bɪk/
argue (v) /'ɑːg.juː/
arrive (v) /ə'raɪv/
art (n) /ɑːt/
beach (n) /biːtʃ/
brush (v) /brʌʃ/
catch (v) /kætʃ/
cereal (n) /'sɪə.ri.əl/
charity (n) /'tʃær.ɪ.ti/
cheeky (adj) /'tʃiː.ki/
cheerful (adj) /'tʃɪə.fəl/
clear (v) /klɪə/
come on (v) /'kʌm.ɒn/
dish (n) /dɪʃ/
evening (n) /'iːv.nɪŋ/
exchange (n) /ɪks'tʃeɪndʒ/
father (n) /'fɑː.ðə/
find out (v) /ˌfaɪnd 'aʊt/
fire (n) /faɪə/
generous (adj) /'dʒen.ər.əs/
hang out (v) /ˌhæŋ.'aʊt/
headphones (n) /'hed.fəʊnz/
hip-hop (n) /'hɪp.hɒp/
honest (adj) /'ɒn.ɪst/
internet (n) /'ɪn.tə.net/
laugh (v) /lɑːf/
lay the table (v) /ˌleɪ ðə 'teɪ.bəl/
lazy (adj) /'leɪ.zi/
lose (v) /luːz/
lovely (adj) /'lʌv.li/
loyal (adj) /'lɔɪ.əl/
meet (v) /miːt/
mp3 player (n) /ˌem.piː'θriː ˌpleɪə/
pay (v) /peɪ/
personality (n) /ˌpɜː.sən'æl.ə.ti/
project (n) /'prɒdʒ.ekt/
roast (adj) /rəʊst/
rubbish (n) /'rʌb.ɪʃ/
sausage (n) /'sɒs.ɪdʒ/
secret (n) /'siː.krət/
share (v) /ʃeə/
short (adj) /ʃɔːt/
smile (n) /smaɪl/
smile (v) /smaɪl/
souvenir (n) /ˌsuː.vən'ɪə/
sports centre (n) /'spɔːts ˌsen.tə/
trust (v) /trʌst/

Unit 2

adult (n) /'æd.ʌlt/
annoyed (adj) /ə'nɔɪd/
antelope (n) /'æn.tɪ.ləʊp/
arrive (v) /ə'raɪv/
awesome (adj) /'ɔː.səm/
badly (adv) /'bæd.li/
baggage reclaim (n) /'bæg.ɪdʒ rɪ'kleɪm/
balcony (n) /'bæl.kə.ni/
battery (n) /'bæt.ər.i/
bowl (n) /bəʊl/
boy (n) /bɔɪ/
camp (n) /kæmp/
cancel (v) /'kæn.səl/
candle (n) /'kæn.dəl/
cartoon (n) /kɑː'tuːn/
chalet (n) /'ʃæl.eɪ/
check-in (n) /'tʃek.ɪn/
cheetah (n) /'tʃiː.tə/
classmate (n) /'klɑːs.meɪt/
coach (n) /kəʊtʃ/
contest (n) /'kɒnt.est/
departure (n) /dɪ'pɑː.tʃə/
disaster (n) /dɪ'zɑː.stə/
expect (v) /ɪk'spekt/
flamingo (n) /flə'mɪŋ.gəʊ/
flat (adj) /flæt/
flight (n) /flaɪt/
flight attendant (n) /'flaɪt ə.ten.dənt/
flower (n) /flaʊə/
fly (v) /flaɪ/
fortunately (adv) /'fɔː.tʃən.ət.li/
gate (n) /geɪt/
guide (n) /gaɪd/
hippopotamus (n) /ˌhɪp.ə'pɒt.ə.məs/
ill (adj) /ɪl/
inbox (n) /'ɪn.bɒks/
incredible (adj) /ɪn'kred.ɪ.bəl/
jam (n) /dʒæm/
jeep (n) /dʒiːp/
journey (n) /'dʒɜː.ni/
leopard (n) /'lep.əd/
lion (n) /laɪ.ən/
loads (n) /ləʊdz/
local (adj) /'ləʊ.kəl/
long (adj) /lɒŋ/
lorry (n) /'lɒr.i/
lose (v) /luːz/
lucky (adj) /'lʌk.i/
motorway (n) /'məʊ.tə.weɪ/
passport (n) /'pɑːs.pɔːt/
passport control (n) /'pɑːs.pɔːt kən.trəʊl/
phone call (n) /'fəʊn ˌkɔːl/
pilot (n) /'paɪ.lət/
poster (n) /'pəʊ.stə/
prize (n) /praɪz/
pyramid (n) /'pɪr.ə.mɪd/
queue (n) /kjuː/

rhino (n) /'raɪ.nəʊ/
rhinoceros (n) /raɪ'nɒs.ər.əs/
runway (n) /'rʌn.weɪ/
safari (n) /sə'fɑː.ri/
season (n) /'siː.zən/
singer (n) /'sɪŋ.ə/
skate park (n) /'skeɪt ˌpɑːk/
special effect (n) /ˌspeʃ.əl ɪ'fekt/
sponsor (v) /'spɒn.sə/
sponsor (n) /'spɒn.sə/
suitcase (n) /'suːt.keɪs/
traffic (n) /'træf.ɪk/
traffic jam (n) /'træf.ɪk ˌdʒæm/
transport (n) /'træn.spɔːt/
tyre (n) /taɪə/
uncomfortable (adj) /ʌn'kʌmf.tə.bəl/
unfortunately (adv) /ʌn'fɔː.tʃən.ətli/
unlucky (adj) /ʌn'lʌk.i/
water (n) /'wɔː.tə/
winter (n) /'wɪn.tə/
wow (excl) /waʊ/
Zambia (n) /'zæm.bi.ə/
zebra (n) /'zeb.rə/

Unit 3

actually (adv) /'æk.tʃuə.li/
admire (v) /əd'maɪə/
afraid (adj) /ə'freɪd/
alive (adj) /ə'laɪv/
ancient (adj) /'eɪn.ʃənt/
archer (n) /'ɑː.tʃə/
army (n) /'ɑː.mi/
attack (v) /ə'tæk/
beat (v) /biːt/
beautiful (adj) /'bjuː.tɪ.fəl/
break out (v) /ˌbreɪk 'aʊt/
Britain (n) /'brɪt.ən/
British (adj) /'brɪt.ɪʃ/
Briton (n) /'brɪt.ən/
broken (adj) /'brəʊ.kən/
Canada (n) /'kæn.ə.də/
catch (v) /kætʃ/
chariot (n) /'tʃær.i.ət/
chess (n) /tʃes/
Chinese (adj) /tʃaɪ'niːz/
clean-up (n) /'kliːn.ʌp/
crash (n) /kræʃ/
cross (adj) /krɒs/
danger (n) /'deɪn.dʒə/
dead (adj) /ded/
disaster (n) /dɪ'zɑː.stə/
dolphin (n) /'dɒl.fɪn/
dragon (n) /'dræg.ən/
drown (v) /draʊn/
earthquake (n) /'ɜːθ.kweɪk/
embarrassed (adj) /ɪm'bær.əst/
enemy (n) /'en.ə.mi/
explosion (n) /ɪk'spləʊ.ʒən/

fault (n) /fɔːlt/
fed up (adj) /ˌfed 'ʌp/
flood (n) /flʌd/
fluently (adv) /'fluː.ənt.li/
glass (n) /glɑːs/
gold (n) /gəʊld/
happiness (n) /'hæpɪ.nəs/
health (n) /helθ/
high (adj) /haɪ/
hit (v) /hɪt/
hurricane (n) /'hʌr.ɪ.kən/
hurry up (v) /ˌhʌr.i 'ʌp/
important (adj) /ɪm'pɔː.tənt/
interview (v) /'ɪn.tə.vjuː/
judo (n) /'dʒuː.dəʊ/
kill (v) /kɪl/
knight (n) /naɪt/
life saver (n) /'laɪf ˌseɪ.və/
magician (n) /mə'dʒɪʃ.ən/
middle (n) /'mɪd.əl/
mysterious (adj) /mɪ'stɪə.ri.əs/
nasty (adj) /'nɑː.sti/
need (v) /niːd/
nothing (n) /'nʌθ.ɪŋ/
occupation (n) /ˌɒk.jə'peɪ.ʃən/
palace (n) /'pæl.ɪs/
phew (excl) /fjuː/
phone (v) /fəʊn/
plastic (adj) /'plæs.tɪk/
poison (n) /'pɔɪ.zən/
power (n) /'paʊ.ə/
princess (n) /prɪn'ses/
pull (v) /pʊl/
queen (n) /kwiːn/
radio (n) /'reɪ.di.əʊ/
raise (v) /reɪz/
real (adj) /rɪəl/
recipe (n) /'res.ɪ.pi/
record player (n) /'rek.ɔːd ˌpleɪə/
relative (n) /'rel.ə.tɪv/
report (n) /rɪ'pɔːt/
rescue (v) /'res.kjuː/
road (n) /rəʊd/
rob (v) /rɒb/
rock 'n' roll (n) /ˌrɒk.ən 'rəʊl/
round (adj) /raʊnd/
rule (v) /ruːl/
safety (n) /'seɪf.ti/
save (v) /seɪv/
sell (v) /sel/
send (v) /send/
shark (n) /ʃɑːk/
sheriff (n) /'ʃer.ɪf/
smell (v) /smel/
smoke (n) /sməʊk/
stone (n) /stəʊn/
stop (v) /stɒp/
strength (n) /streŋθ/
sugar (n) /'ʃʊg.ə/
surfboard (n) /'sɜːf.bɔːd/
swimmer (n) /'swɪm.ə/
sword (n) /sɔːd/
talented (adj) /'tæl.ən.tɪd/
taste (v) /teɪst/

tax (n) /tæks/
teen (adj) /tiːn/
teenager (n) /'tiːnˌeɪ.dʒə/
thief (n) /θiːf/
ticket (n) /'tɪk.ɪt/
tribe (n) /traɪb/
unhappy (adj) /ʌn'hæp.i/
upset (adj) /ʌp'set/
USA (n) /ˌjuː.es'eɪ/
washing machine (n) /'wɒʃ.ɪŋ
    məˌʃiːn/
wave (n) /weɪv/
whale (n) /weɪl/
win (v) /wɪn/
worried (adj) /'wʌ.rid/

Unit 4

Antarctica (n) /æn'tɑːk.tɪ.kə/
anyway (adv) /'en.i.weɪ/
Arctic (n) /'ɑːk.tɪk/
area (n) /'eə.ri.ə/
bat (n) /bæt/
beak (n) /biːk/
bear (n) /beə/
bench (n) /bentʃ/
better (adj) /'bet.ə/
bigger (adj) /'bɪg.ə/
biggest (adj) /'bɪg.ɪst/
can (n) /kæn/
careful (adj) /'keə.fəl/
carefully (adv) /'keə.fəli/
chewing gum (n) /'tʃuː.ɪŋ
    ˌɡʌm/
Chile (n) /'tʃɪl.i/
chill out (v) /ˌtʃɪl 'aʊt/
claw (n) /klɔː/
collection (n) /kə'lek.ʃən/
congratulations (excl)
    /kənˌɡrætʃ.ə'leɪ.ʃənz/
cousin (n) /'kʌz.ən/
cricket (n) /'krɪk.ɪt/
crowded (adj) /'kraʊ.dɪd/
cut (v) /kʌt/
deep (adj) /diːp/
dig (v) /dɪɡ/
dirtier (adj) /'dɜː.ti.ə/
dirtiest (adj) /'dɜː.ti.ɪst/
dirty (adj) /'dɜː.ti/
drier (adj) /'draɪ.ə/
driest (adj) /'draɪ.ɪst/
dry (adj) /draɪ/
easier (adj) /'iː.zi.ə/
easiest (adj) /'iː.zi.ɪst/
Europe (n) /'jʊə.rəp/
expert (n) /'ek.spɜːt/
far (adv) /fɑː/
faster (adj) /'fɑːst.ə/
fastest (adj) /'fɑːst.ɪst/
feather (n) /'feð.ə/
fence (n) /fens/
fit (adj) /fɪt/
four-pack (n) /'fɔː ˌpæk/
friendlier (adj) /'frend.li.ə/
friendliest (adj) /'frend.li.ɪst/
full (adj) /fʊl/

funnier (adj) /'fʌni.ə/
funniest (adj) /'fʌni.ɪst/
fur (n) /fɜː/
further (adj) /'fɜː.ðə/
furthest (adj) /'fɜː.ðɪst/
hamster (n) /'hæm.stə/
happier (adj) /'hæpi.ə/
happiest (adj) /'hæpi.ɪst/
heavier (adj) /'hevi.ə/
heavy (adj) /'hev.i/
higher (adj) /haɪə/
highest (adj) /'haɪ.ɪst/
hoof (n) /huːf/
hooves (n) /huːvz/
hotter (adj) /'hɒtə/
hottest (adj) /'hɒt.ɪst/
howler monkey (n) /'haʊ.lə
    ˌmʌŋ.ki/
hungriest (adj) /'hʌŋ.gri.ɪst/
hurt (v) /hɜːt/
intelligent (adj) /ɪn'tel.ɪ.dʒənt/
Japan (n) /dʒə'pæn/
jungle (n) /'dʒʌŋ.ɡəl/
keep clean (v) /ˌkiːp 'kliːn/
king cobra (n) /ˌkɪŋ 'kəʊ.brə/
longer (adj) /ˌlɒŋg.ə/
longest (adj) /ˌlɒŋg.ɪst/
marine (adj) /mə'riːn/
monkey (n) /'mʌŋ.ki/
nature (n) /'neɪ.tʃə/
neighbour (n) /'neɪ.bə/
nicer (adj) /'naɪs.ə/
noisier (adj) /'nɔɪ.zi.ə/
older (adj) /'əʊld.ə/
opinion (n) /ə'pɪn.jən/
opposite (adj) /'ɒp.ə.zɪt/
organise (adj) /'ɔː.gən.aɪz/
path (n) /pɑːθ/
pay (v) /peɪ/
plant (n) /plɑːnt/
point (n) /pɔɪnt/
poisonous (adj) /'pɔɪ.zən.əs/
pond (n) /pɒnd/
popular (adj) /'pɒp.jə.lə/
pot (n) /pɒt/
recycle (v) /riː'saɪ.kəl/
ring (n) /rɪŋ/
risk (n) /rɪsk/
romantic (adj) /rəʊ'mæn.tɪk/
safest (adj) /'seɪf.ɪst/
scissors (n) /'sɪz.əz/
shorter (adj) /'ʃɔː.tə/
shortest (adj) /'ʃɔːt.ɪst/
Siberia (n) /saɪ'bɪə.ri.ə/
sick (adj) /sɪk/
smallest (adj) /'smɔːl.ɪst/
snack (n) /snæk/
snail (n) /sneɪl/
South America (n) /ˌsaʊθ
    ə'mer.ɪ.kə/
stomach (n) /'stʌm.ək/
stronger (adj) /'strɒŋg.ə/
stuck (adj) /stʌk/
study (v) /'stʌd.i/
tail (n) /teɪl/
teeth (n) /tiːθ/
throw (v) /θrəʊ/

tooth (n) /tuːθ/
tortoise (n) /'tɔː.təs/
unfair (adj) /ʌn'feə/
unfit (adj) /ʌn'fɪt/
unfriendly (adj) /ʌn'frend.li/
unkind (adj) /ʌn'kaɪnd/
unpopular (adj) /ʌn'pɒp.jə.lə/
unsafe (adj) /ʌn'seɪf/
unwell (adj) /ʌn'wel/
volcano (n) /vɒl'keɪ.nəʊ/
wet (adj) /wet/
wettest (adj) /'wet.ɪst/
wide (adj) /waɪd/
wildlife (n) /'waɪld.laɪf/
wing (n) /wɪŋ/
worse (adj) /wɜːs/
worst (adj) /wɜːst/
yoghurt (n) /'jɒɡ.ət/
young (adj) /jʌŋ/

Unit 5

agent (n) /'eɪ.dʒənt/
beef (n) /biːf/
butcher (n) /'bʊtʃ.ə/
calculator (n) /'kæl.kjə.leɪ.tə/
Christmas (n) /'krɪs.məs/
credit card (n) /'kred.ɪt ˌkɑːd/
dictionary (n) /'dɪk.ʃən.ri/
fancy dress (adj) /ˌfæn.si
    'dres/
festival (n) /'fes.tɪ.vəl/
fixed (adj) /fɪkst/
greengrocer (n)
    /'griːnˌɡrəʊ.sə/
greeting (n) /'griː.tɪŋ/
hey (excl) /heɪ/
huge (adj) /hjuːdʒ/
ice skating (n) /'aɪs ˌskeɪ.tɪŋ/
in fact (exp) /ˌɪn 'fækt/
indoors (adv) /ˌɪn'dɔːz/
invitation (n) /ɪn.vɪ'teɪ.ʃən/
make-up (n) /'meɪk.ʌp/
mate (n) /meɪt/
medicine (n) /'med.sən/
medieval (adj) /ˌmed.i'iː.vəl/
memory card (n) /'mem.ər.i
    ˌkɑːd/
multiplex (n) /'mʌl.tɪ.pleks/
newsagent (n)
    /'njuːzˌeɪ.dʒənt/
orchestra (n) /'ɔː.kɪ.strə/
outdoors (adv) /ˌaʊt'dɔːz/
permission (n) /pə'mɪʃ.ən/
pharmacy (n) /'fɑː.mə.si/
price (n) /praɪs/
punctuation (n)
    /ˌpʌŋk.tʃu'eɪ.ʃən/
reason (n) /'riː.zən/
refuse (v) /rɪf'juːz/
reply (v) /rɪ'plaɪ/
rude (adj) /ruːd/
slide (n) /slaɪd/
slope (n) /sləʊp/
spelling (n) /'spel.ɪŋ/
stadium (n) /'steɪ.di.əm/

store (n) /stɔː/
stranger (n) /'streɪn.dʒə/
surprised (adj) /sə'praɪzd/
take care (excl) /ˌteɪk 'keə/
tennis racquet (n) /'ten.ɪs
    ˌræk.ɪt/
trophy (n) /'trəʊ.fi/
weekly (adj) /'wiː.kli/

Unit 6

abbreviation (n)
    /əˌbriː.vi'eɪ.ʃən/
action (n) /'æk.ʃən/
alone (adj) /ə'ləʊn/
approximately (adv)
    /ə'prɒk.sɪ.mət.li/
attachment (n) /ə'tætʃ.mənt/
average (adj) /'æv.ər.ɪdʒ/
board game (n) /'bɔːd ˌgeɪm/
canteen (n) /kæn'tiːn/
cheer up (v) /ˌtʃɪər 'ʌp/
chore (n) /tʃɔː/
comedy (n) /'kɒm.ə.di/
confuse (v) /kən'fjuːz/
confused (adj) /kən'fjuːzd/
contestant (n) /kən'tes.tənt/
cursor (n) /'kɜː.sə/
delete (v) /dɪ'liːt/
depressed (adj) /dɪ'prest/
depressing (adj) /dɪ'pres.ɪŋ/
detail (n) /'diː.teɪl/
disgusted (adj) /dɪs'gʌst.ɪd/
disgusting (adj) /dɪs'gʌst.ɪŋ/
download (v) /ˌdaʊn'ləʊd/
embarrassed (adj)
    /ɪm'bær.əst/
emoticon (n) /ɪ'məʊ.tɪ.kɒn/
helmet (n) /'hel.mət/
icon (n) /'aɪ.kɒn/
immediately (adv) /ɪ'miː.di.ət.li/
improve (v) /ɪm'pruːv/
instead (adv) /ɪn'sted/
irritated (adj) /'ɪr.ɪ.teɪ.tɪd/
irritating (adj) /'ɪr.ɪ.teɪ.tɪŋ/
joystick (n) /'dʒɔɪ.stɪk/
leader (n) /'liː.də/
madness (n) /'mæd.nəs/
mark (n) /mɑːk/
Merry Christmas (excl)
    /ˌmer.i 'krɪs.məs/
messaging (n) /'mes.ɪdʒ.ɪŋ/
monitor (n) /'mɒn.ɪ.tə/
mouse mat (n) /'maʊs ˌmæt/
nervous (adj) /'nɜː.vəs/
New Zealand (n)
    /ˌnjuː'ziː.lənd/
notebook (n) /'nəʊt.bʊk/
open (v) /'əʊ.pən/
order (v) /'ɔː.də/
pal (n) /pæl/
photo story (n) /'fəʊ.təʊ
    ˌstɔː.ri/
plug (n) /plʌɡ/
printer (n) /'prɪn.tə/
reality show (n) /ri'æl.ə.ti ˌʃəʊ/

receive *(v)* /rɪˈsiːv/
register *(v)* /ˈredʒ.ɪ.stə/
research *(n)* /rɪˈsɜːtʃ/
sms *(n)* /ˌes.emˈes/
soap opera *(n)* /ˈsəʊp.ɒp.rə/
staff *(n)* /stɑːf/
stand for *(v)* /ˈstænd ˌfɔː/
talent show *(n)* /ˈtæl.ənt ˌʃəʊ/
text *(v)* /tekst/
the Philippines *(n)* /ðə
 ˈfɪl.ɪ.piːnz/
tray *(n)* /treɪ/
vet *(n)* /vet/

Unit 7

accident *(n)* /ˈæk.sɪ.dənt/
advert *(n)* /ˈæd.vɜːt/
asleep *(adv)* /əˈsliːp/
bright *(adj)* /braɪt/
burglar *(n)* /ˈbɜː.glə/
busily *(adv)* /ˈbɪz.ɪ.li/
crash *(v)* /kræʃ/
creature *(n)* /ˈkriː.tʃə/
design *(v)* /dɪˈzaɪn/
destination *(n)* /ˌdes.tɪˈneɪ.ʃən/
destroy *(v)* /dɪˈstrɔɪ/
distance *(n)* /ˈdɪs.təns/
electricity *(n)* /ˌel.ɪkˈtrɪs.ɪ.ti/
exist *(v)* /ɪgˈzɪst/
footprint *(n)* /ˈfʊt.prɪnt/
frozen *(adj)* /ˈfrəʊ.zən/
gig *(n)* /gɪg/
happily *(adv)* /ˈhæp.ɪ.li/
instruction *(n)* /ɪnˈstrʌk.ʃən/
jog *(v)* /dʒɒg/
journalist *(n)* /ˈdʒɜː.nəl.ɪst/
land *(v)* /lænd/
latest *(adj)* /ˈleɪ.tɪst/
leaflet *(n)* /ˈliː.flət/
lift *(v)* /lɪft/
manual *(adj)* /ˈmæn.ju.əl/
milk *(n)* /mɪlk/
nervously *(adv)* /ˈnɜː.vəs.li/
newspaper *(n)* /ˈnjuːsˌpeɪ.pə/
notice *(v)* /ˈnəʊ.tɪs/
offer *(v)* /ˈɒf.ə/
organise *(v)* /ˈɔː.gən.aɪz/
police officer *(n)* /pəˈliːs
 ˌɒf.ɪ.sə/
poster *(n)* /ˈpəʊ.stə/
power cut *(n)* /ˈpaʊ.ə ˌkʌt/
print *(v)* /prɪnt/
seaside *(n)* /ˈsiː.saɪd/
shine *(v)* /ʃaɪn/
sink *(v)* /sɪŋk/
sunglasses *(n)* /ˈsʌnˌglɑː.sɪz/
truck *(n)* /trʌk/
wolf *(n)* /wʊlf/
wooden *(adj)* /ˈwʊd.ən/
yeti *(n)* /ˈjet.i/
yoga *(n)* /ˈjəʊ.gə/

Unit 8

ambition *(n)* /æmˈbɪʃ.ən/

astronaut *(n)* /ˈæs.trə.nɔːt/
athlete *(n)* /ˈæθ.liːt/
audience *(n)* /ˈɔː.di.əns/
blow *(v)* /bləʊ/
bridge *(n)* /brɪdʒ/
cello *(n)* /ˈtʃel.əʊ/
charity *(n)* /ˈtʃær.ɪ.ti/
cloud *(n)* /klaʊd/
clown *(n)* /klaʊn/
comedian *(n)* /kəˈmiː.di.ən/
compete *(v)* /kəmˈpiːt/
dentist *(n)* /ˈden.tɪst/
detective *(n)* /dɪˈtek.tɪv/
director *(n)* /daɪˈrek.tə/
dream *(v)* /driːm/
driver *(n)* /ˈdraɪ.və/
drummer *(n)* /ˈdrʌm.ə/
educate *(v)* /ˈedʒ.ʊ.keɪt/
education *(n)* /ˌedʒ.ʊˈkeɪ.ʃən/
engineer *(n)* /ˌen.dʒɪˈnɪə/
fire fighter *(n)* /ˈfaɪə.faɪt.ə/
flute *(n)* /fluːt/
footballer *(n)* /ˈfʊt.bɔː.lə/
get fit *(v)* /ˌget ˈfɪt/
handmade *(adj)* /ˌhændˈmeɪd/
hang on *(v)* /ˈhæŋ ˌɒn/
instrument *(n)* /ˈɪn.strə.mənt/
joke *(n)* /dʒəʊk/
ladder *(n)* /ˈlæd.ə/
lady *(n)* /ˈleɪ.di/
laughter *(n)* /ˈlɑːf.tə/
magic *(n)* /ˈmædʒ.ɪk/
musician *(n)* /mjuːˈzɪʃ.ən/
nightmare *(n)* /ˈnaɪt.meə/
no worries *(exp)* /ˈnəʊ ˌwʌriz/
nurse *(n)* /nɜːs/
obvious *(adj)* /ˈɒb.vi.əs/
organisation *(n)*
 /ˌɔː.gən.aɪˈzeɪ.ʃən/
pair *(n)* /peə/
peak *(n)* /piːk/
per cent *(adv)* /pəˈsent/
poverty *(n)* /ˈpɒv.ə.ti/
pyjamas *(n)* /pɪˈdʒɑː.məz/
racing driver *(n)* /ˈreɪ.sɪŋ
 ˌdraɪ.və/
recorder *(n)* /rɪˈkɔː.də/
saxophone *(n)* /ˈsæk.sə.fəʊn/
scientist *(n)* /ˈsaɪ.ən.tɪst/
silence *(n)* /ˈsaɪ.ləns/
single *(adj)* /ˈsɪŋ.gəl/
skateboard *(v)* /ˈskeɪt.bɔːd/
solve *(v)* /sɒlv/
stamp *(n)* /stæmp/
string *(n)* /strɪŋ/
success *(n)* /səkˈses/
superhero *(n)* /ˈsuː.pəˌhɪə.rəʊ/
Tanzania *(n)* /ˌtæn.zəˈniː.ə/
term *(n)* /tɜːm/
toothache *(n)* /ˈtuː.θ.eɪk/
total *(n)* /ˈtəʊ.təl/
traditional *(adj)* /trəˈdɪʃ.ən.əl/
trumpet *(n)* /ˈtrʌm.pɪt/
tunnel *(n)* /ˈtʌn.əl/
umbrella *(n)* /ʌmˈbrel.ə/
university *(n)* /ˌjuː.nɪˈvɜː.sə.ti/
van *(n)* /væn/

viewer *(n)* /vjuːə/
violin *(n)* /ˌvaɪ.əˈlɪn/
voice *(n)* /vɔɪs/
writer *(n)* /ˈraɪ.tə/

Unit 9

advanced *(adj)* /ədˈvɑːnst/
animation *(n)* /ˌæn.ɪˈmeɪ.ʃən/
apartment *(n)* /əˈpɑːt.mənt/
artificial intelligence *(n)*
 /ˌɑː.tɪˈfɪʃ.əl ɪnˈtel.ɪ.dʒəns/
body *(n)* /ˈbɒd.i/
bottom *(n)* /ˈbɒt.əm/
brain *(n)* /breɪn/
calm down *(v)* /ˌkɑːm ˈdaʊn/
camper van *(n)* /ˈkæm.pə
 ˌvæn/
choice *(n)* /tʃɔɪs/
click *(v)* /klɪk/
clue *(n)* /kluː/
confession *(n)* /kənˈfeʃ.ən/
connect *(v)* /kəˈnekt/
console *(n)* /ˈkɒn.səʊl/
container *(n)* /kənˈteɪ.nə/
control *(v)* /kənˈtrəʊl/
decision *(n)* /dɪˈsɪʒ.ən/
discover *(v)* /dɪˈskʌv.ə/
document *(n)* /ˈdɒk.jʊ.mənt/
dwarf *(adj)* /dwɔːf/
enter *(v)* /ˈen.tə/
environment *(n)*
 /ɪnˈvaɪə.rən.mənt/
experience *(n)* /ɪkˈspɪə.ri.əns/
explain *(v)* /ɪkˈspleɪn/
explore *(v)* /ɪkˈsplɔː/
extreme *(adj)* /ɪkˈstriːm/
factory *(n)* /ˈfæk.tər.i/
file *(n)* /faɪl/
folder *(n)* /ˈfəʊl.də/
game console *(n)* /ˈgeɪm
 ˌkɒn.səʊl/
guard *(v)* /gɑːd/
hole *(n)* /həʊl/
hospital *(n)* /ˈhɒs.pɪ.təl/
human being *(n)* /ˌhjuː.mən
 ˈbiː.ɪŋ/
impossible *(adj)* /ɪmˈpɒs.ɪ.bəl/
Jupiter *(n)* /ˈdʒuː.pɪ.tə/
laptop *(n)* /ˈlæp.tɒp/
married *(adj)* /ˈmær.id/
Mars *(n)* /mɑːz/
Mercury *(n)* /ˈmɜː.kjʊr.i/
metal *(n)* /ˈmet.əl/
miss *(v)* /mɪs/
national *(adj)* /ˈnæʃ.ən.əl/
oxygen *(n)* /ˈɒk.sɪ.dʒən/
pass *(v)* /pɑːs/
password *(n)* /ˈpɑːs.wɜːd/
perfect *(adj)* /ˈpɜː.fɪkt/
Pluto *(n)* /ˈpluː.təʊ/
pollution *(n)* /pəˈluː.ʃən/
press *(v)* /pres/
puzzle *(n)* /ˈpʌz.əl/
recognise *(v)* /ˈrek.əg.naɪz/
remote control *(n)* /rɪˌməʊt.

kənˈtrəʊl/
restart *(v)* /ˌriːˈstɑːt/
Saturn *(n)* /ˈsæt.ən/
save *(v)* /seɪv/
screensaver *(n)*
 /ˈskriːn.seɪ.və/
scroll *(v)* /skrəʊl/
smart *(adj)* /smɑːt/
solar system *(n)* /ˈsəʊ.lə ˌsɪs.
 təm/
survive *(v)* /səˈvaɪv/
technology *(n)* /tekˈnɒl.ə.dʒi/
temperature *(n)* /ˈtem.prɪ.tʃə/
time capsule *(n)* /ˈtaɪm
 ˌkæp.sjuːl/
Uranus *(n)* /jəˈreɪn.əs/
vacuum *(v)* /ˈvæk.juːm/
web page *(n)* /ˈweb ˌpeɪdʒ/

Unit 10

achieve *(v)* /əˈtʃiːv/
achievement *(n)* /əˈtʃiːv.mənt/
badminton *(n)* /ˈbæd.mɪn.tən/
bake *(v)* /beɪk/
basic *(adj)* /ˈbeɪ.sɪk/
biography *(n)* /baɪˈɒg.rə.fi/
black belt *(n)* /ˈblæk ˌbelt/
BMX ™ *(n)* /ˌbiː.emˈeks/
career *(n)* /kəˈrɪə/
championship *(n)*
 /ˈtʃæm.pi.ən.ʃɪp/
disagree *(v)* /ˌdɪs.əˈgriː/
divorce *(v)* /dɪˈvɔːs/
episode *(n)* /ˈep.ɪ.səʊd/
European *(adj)* /ˌjʊə.rəˈpiː.ən/
fluid *(n)* /ˈfluː.ɪd/
general knowledge *(n)*
 /ˌdʒen.ər.əl ˈnɒl.ɪdʒ/
go-kart *(n)* /ˈgəʊ.kɑːt/
honey *(n)* /ˈhʌn.i/
injury *(n)* /ˈɪn.dʒər.i/
inspiration *(n)* /ˌɪn.spɪrˈeɪ.ʃən/
junior *(adj)* /ˈdʒuː.nɪə/
karting *(n)* /ˈkɑːt.ɪŋ/
lucky charm *(n)* /ˌlʌk.i ˈtʃɑːm/
marathon *(n)* /ˈmær.ə.θən/
medal *(n)* /ˈmed.əl/
nickname *(n)* /ˈnɪk.neɪm/
once *(adv)* /wʌns/
owner *(n)* /ˈəʊn.ə/
perform *(v)* /pəˈfɔːm/
philosophy *(n)* /fɪˈlɒs.ə.fi/
Portugal *(n)* /ˈpɔː.tʃə.gəl/
positive *(adj)* /ˈpɒz.ə.tɪv/
president *(n)* /ˈprez.ɪ.dənt/
race *(n)* /reɪs/
radio-controlled *(adj)*
 /ˈreɪ.di.əʊ kənˌtrəʊld/
reggae *(n)* /ˈreg.eɪ/
score *(v)* /skɔː/
scorpion *(n)* /ˈskɔː.pi.ən/
season *(n)* /ˈsiː.zən/
shake *(v)* /ʃeɪk/
shame *(n)* /ʃeɪm/
spare *(adj)* /speə/

speed *(n)* /spiːd/
spider *(n)* /ˈspaɪ.də/
sporting *(adj)* /spɔːt.ɪŋ/
stepmother *(n)* /ˈstepˌmʌð.ə/
suggestion *(n)* /səˈdʒes.tʃən/
support *(n)* /səˈpɔːt/
sure *(adv)* /ʃɔː/
swap *(v)* /swɒp/
trophy *(n)* /ˈtrəʊ.fi/
Twitter ™ *(n)* /ˈtwɪt.ə/
youngest *(adj)* /ˈjʌŋɡ.ɪst

Thanks and Acknowledgements

The authors and publishers would like to thank the teachers who commented on the material at different stages of its development, the teachers who allowed us to observe their classes, and those who gave up their valuable time for interviews and focus groups.

The authors would like to thank all the people who have worked so hard on *Your Space*. We are especially grateful to James Dingle for inviting us to write this project and for his support during all stages of its development. We would also like to thank Frances Amrani, commissioning editor, and the editors Claire Powell, Rosemary Bradley and Ruth Bell-Pellegrini for their skilled editorial contributions, perceptive editing, and commitment to the project; the design team at Wild Apple; David Lawton for his design ideas; Emma Szlachta for her excellent project management and Graham Avery, production manager, for his support. We are grateful to all the other writers on the project for their creative input. We would also like to thank the many reviewers and teachers who contributed to the development of this course. We extend a special thank you to the editor Rachael Gibbon for her unwavering focus during the development process.

The publishers acknowledge the following sources of copyright material and are grateful for the permissions granted. While every effort has been made, it has not always been possible to identify the sources of all material used, or to trace all copyright holders. If any omissions are brought to our notice, we will be happy to include the appropriate acknowledgements on reprinting.

Photo Acknowledgements.

p. 8 Geoff du Feu/Alamy p. 10 Frédéric Soltan/Corbis p. 11T DoorstepBus.Org p. 11B oliveromg/Shutterstock p. 13 (Shakespeare) c./Shutterstock p. 13 (Jackson) Steve Double, Camera Press London p. 13 (de Vinci) Elena Korn/Shutterstock p. 13 (Curie) photos.com/Thinkstock p. 13 (Chaplin) SuperStock p. 13 (Pele) INTERPHOTO/Alamy p. 15 Christian Lazzari/Shutterstock p. 18TL tropicalpix/iStock p. 18TR Kevin Tavares/iStock p. 18BL Steve Allan/iStock p. 18BR Photolibrary Group/Robert Harding Travel/Marco Simoni p. 19 Feng Yu/Shutterstock p. 26 Science & Society Picture Library/NASA pp. 29 (hippo, ostrich, cheetah), 35 Eric Isselée/Shutterstock p. 29 (Thames) Richard Cooke/Alamy p. 29 (Nile) Peter de Clercq/Alamy p. 29 (Tokyo) bluehand/Shutterstock p. 29 (Amsterdam) Eugene Suslo/Shutterstock p. 29 (rollerblades) nito/Shutterstock p. 29 (bike) hamurishi/Shutterstock p. 29 (tortoise) fivespots/Shutterstock p. 29 (beach) iStockphoto/Thinkstock p. 29 (Antarctica) RIA NOVOSTI/Science Photo Library p. 30TL guillermo77/Shutterstock p. 30TR Gina Sanders/Shutterstock p. 30BL Ablestock.com/Thinkstock p. 30BR Mlenny/iStock pp. 37, 61 Monkey Business Images/Shutterstock p. 42a William Caram/Alamy p. 42b Universal/The Kobal Collection p. 42c Mary Evans Picture Library p. 42d Jeremy Pembrey/Alamy p. 42e Tony Hobbs/Alamy p. 42f Rex Features p. 43 Tupungato/Shutterstock p. 46 Arlene Treiber/Shutterstock p. 46 Juan Carlos Tinjaca/Shutterstock p. 50 (Paul) Comstock/Thinkstock pp. 50 (Izzie, Amelia), 53 Jupiterimages/Thinkstock p. 50 (Alfie) Pixland/Thinkstock p. 50 (Daniel) Goodshoot RF/Thinkstock p. 52 Bill Noll/iStock p. 66 Adam Woolfitt/Corbis p. 67 Allstar Picture Library/Alamy p. 72 holbox/Shutterstock p. 74 Yuri Arcurs/Shutterstock p. 75 Sergey Kamshylin/Shutterstock p. 79 (storm) loflo69/Shutterstock p. 79 (elephant) Richard Peterson/Shutterstock p. 79 (Nelson's Column) Graham Tomlin/Shutterstock p. 79 (London Eye) photogl/Shutterstock p. 79 (Big Ben) PeterSVETphoto/Shutterstock p. 79 (Earhart) Science, Industry & Business Library/New York Public Library/Science Photo Library p. 82T United Archives GmbH/Alamy p. 82L fstock/Shutterstock p. 82R hartphotography/Shutterstock p. 82B Melissa Moseley/Sony Pictures/Bureau L.A. Collection/Corbis p. 83T Fred Stein, Camera Press London p. 83B Lasse Kristensen/Shutterstock

Artwork Acknowledgements

Adrian Barclay (*Beehive Illustration*) pp. 6L, 8T, 24, 32B, 37, 44, 64T,L, 69R, 78; Andrew Hennessey pp. 54, 70T; Andy Parker pp. 68, 74, 75, 79; Carl Pearce pp. 17, 25, 33, 41, 49B, 50, 57, 65B, 73, 81; David Benham (*Graham Cameron Illustration*) pp. 4, 8, 14T, 21L, 23T, 34, 41, 47, 56, 60, 63; Emmanuel Cerisier (*Beehive Illustration*) pp. 80; Graeme Reid pp. 58; Humberto Blanco (*Sylvie poggio*) pp. 16, 20, 28T, 53, 64BR, 65T, 69T,L, 71, 76; Jo Taylor pp. 6R, 15, 40, 45, 55B, 61; Laszlo Veres (*Beehive Illustration*) pp. 14B; Matt Ward (*Beehive Illustration*) pp. 5, 11, 22R, 23B, 28B, 39T, 48, 49T, 62L, 70L, 72, 79; Simon Rumble (*Beehive Illustration*) pp. 7B, 21R, 22L, 27, 32T, 38, 39B, 55T, 62R; Wild Apple Design pp. 79(emoticon)

The publishers would like to extend a warm thanks to all the teachers and freelance collaborators who have made a valuable contribution to this material.